KAREN YORK

PHOTOGRAPHS BY PADDY WALES

The Holistic Garden

CREATING SPACES FOR HEALTH AND HEALING

Prentice
Hall
Canada

A Pearson Company

TORONTO

Canadian Cataloguing in Publication Data

York, Karen

      The holistic garden : Creating spaces for health and healing

ISBN 0-13-060659-2

1. Gardening—Psychological aspects. 2. Gardening—Therapeutic use. 3. Gardening. I. Wales, Paddy, 1951–
II. Title.

SB453.5.Y67 2001   635'.01'9   C2001-901239-X

ISBN 0-13-060659-2

Editorial Director, Trade Division: Andrea Crozier
Acquisitions Editor: Andrea Crozier
Managing Editor: Tracy Bordian
Copy Editor: Nancy Carroll
Proofreader: Rachelle Redford
Art Direction: Mary Opper
Cover Design: Gary Beelik
Interior Design: Mary Opper/Jennifer Federico
Cover Image: Photodisk
Author Photograph: Andreas Trauttmansdorff
Production Manager: Kathrine Pummell
Page Layout: Kyle Gell Design

1 2 3 4 5 WEB 05 04 03 02 01
Printed and bound in Canada.

ATTENTION: CORPORATIONS

Books are available at quantity discounts with bulk purchase for educational, business, or sales promotional use.
For information, please email or write to: Pearson PTR Canada, Special Sales, PTR Division, 26 Prince Andrew
Place, Don Mills, Ontario, M3C 2T8. Email **ss.corp@pearsoned.com.** Please supply: title of book, ISBN, quantity, how the book will be used, date needed.

Visit the Pearson PTR Canada Web site! Send us your comments, browse our catalogues, and more.
www.pearsonptr.ca

Prentice
Hall
Canada

A Pearson Company

For Lisa,
who set me on this path

CONTENTS

ACKNOWLEDGMENTS

Like everything in life, this book is part of a chain of cause and effect. Among those who caused me to ask the questions (and who provided many answers) are the vastly knowledgeable Henry Kock and Martin Galloway. Giving me equal cause for thanks are Marjorie Harris, who was unbelievably generous with encouragement, e-mails and plants alike; the cheerful pursuer of pollen, Thomas Ogren; David Nowak of the USDA Forest Service; Ross Barrable of Soundscapes International; Monica Kuhn of Toronto's Rooftop Gardens Resource Group; Royal Botanical Gardens librarian, Linda Brownlee; gardener/illustrator, Diane Rhoades; Felicity Lukace and the residents of Baycrest Terrace; the many members of the Canadian Horticultural Therapy Association and the American Horticultural Therapy Association who shared their knowledge and experiences; the folks at City Farmer; Paddy Wales, who translated my words into glorious visuals; Andrea Crozier and Tracy Bordian at Pearson PTR Canada; Nancy Carroll, who brought to bear a gardener's love and an editor's skill on this manuscript; my mother, who has always lighted my way and, of course, my true "soil mate," my husband, Silvio. The effects of all can be found in these pages.

Heartfelt thanks to the following who generously welcomed Paddy Wales and her camera into their gardens: Geri Barnes, Ann Buffam, Joanie and Fred Carter, Marian Clarke, Ellen de Man, Sue Evanetz, Nori Fletcher, Pam Frost, Shirley Hebenton, Elizabeth Litherland, Kathy Leishman, Bruce McConnell, Phoebe Noble, Glen Patterson, Clare Philips, George Radford, Joe and Jo Ronsley, Judy Walker, Bill Walter, Nancy Webber, Stuart Webber; Hollyhock Farm, Park & Tilford Gardens, University of British Columbia Botanical Garden, VanDusen Botanical Garden, and Westridge Farms.

THE GREEN CONNECTION

He who knows what sweets and virtues are in the ground, the plants, the waters, the heavens, and how to come at these enchantments, is the rich and royal man.

RALPH WALDO EMERSON,

NATURE, 1844

I remember lying in my bed as a child, imagining my place or "address"—my bed, my room, my house, my street, my neighborhood, my town, my province, my country, my continent, the earth, the Milky Way, the universe—until my mind couldn't go any further. Then I'd think of the vast millions of people and creatures who had lived before and were living elsewhere on this planet and, while it was frightening to think of myself as an infinitesimal speck of sand (and probably not as long lived), there was also a peculiarly thrilling kind of frisson. Today, that childish fear has grown into a deep feeling of awe at the forces that knit air, water and dust into a complex skein of life whose richness and diversity we've only begun to understand.

It is this intricate web that sustains us, from the teeming bacteria in a teaspoon of soil to the rolling oceans and misty rain forests. But in our self-important rush through modern life, we have lost our sense of place, and not just broken our connection with the land but damaged it severely. Our health is inextricably bound to the earth's health that we have jeopardized; the good news is that, in restoring the earth, we restore ourselves. The garden, as Peter Harper so eloquently puts it, "provides a unique opportunity to explore the mutual healing between you and the Earth. It is a model of the universe, a microcosm of the biosphere and a metaphor for yourself." [1]

I have wrestled somewhat with that word, *healing*, because for many, and according to the first dictionary definition, it is synonymous with *cure*. I prefer the second meaning: "to set right," as in "to heal the rift between us." If we grow in understanding and set things right with nature in our gardens, then we too can be "set right," and the rifts in our lives, whether with our family, our work or within ourselves, will be healed. There is a third, equally essential definition of healing: "to restore a person to spiritual wholeness." That is something we all strive for—and can achieve, despite disease or disability.

Whether consciously or not, we know the healing power of nature: it's what drives us into our gardens to dig in the earth, revel in a bed of peonies and flaunt our dirty fingernails as a badge of honor. It's what sends city people on weekend traffic marathons to the cottage, or compels us to seek out the nearest sheltering tree or patch of greenery when we are stressed. As we better understand the *why* and *how* of nature's healing powers, we will see that the prescription calls for a more holistic approach. Just as holistic medicine requires looking at the whole person (body, mind, emotions and environment), so we need to look at all the elements of nature (flora, fauna, air, water and soil) and understand how they fit together. Nothing in nature happens in isolation. You're not setting anything right if, when you see a few aphids on your roses, you start blasting them with a chemical spray. That's like breaking an egg into a bowl and expecting to make a cake, with no other ingredients, with no mixing or baking.

Like each one of us, nature is constantly striving to achieve balance out of constant upset, from an earthquake shattering a coastal ecosystem to a bacterial invasion of a single tree. We wrestle with balancing the rational and the emotional, the spiritual and the secular, our work and our home, our need for solitude and our desire for company—for in balance lies harmony. And to achieve that, even briefly, is to be filled with the exquisite sense that all is right with the world.

This is not to say that nature is benign; there is danger in anthropomorphizing, in depicting "Mother Nature" as some maternal figure in gingham and a straw hat. The earth nurtures and sustains us, but the natural world is an ongoing battle for survival, full of violence, sex and alien beauty, from the single-celled bacteria with a 30-minute lifespan, to the 1,000-year-old redwood. And nature can be

To look into the heart of a flower is to know the healing power of nature, and to realize that in restoring the health of the earth, we restore ourselves.

dangerous: some of the most virulent poisons known come from plants (*ricin* from the castor bean, *coniine* from poison hemlock and *solanine* from the tomato/potato family). Nature can also be utterly unforgiving, which is why gardeners shriek and moan when downpours flatten the peonies just as they reach their full blowsy glory, when caterpillars defoliate the prize rose, when tomatoes blacken and fall off the vine in a pile of mush. This is why gardeners are constantly urged to work with nature, not against it.

The notion of nature as adversary misses the point; it is not a question of us against them (or it). Nature isn't something "out there" that we visit occasionally or contend with or control. Nature is us and we are nature. We are simply one thread in the web of life. As the Human Genome Project, a colossal effort to map our genetic makeup, has revealed, half of a human's 30,000 to 40,000 genes are related to those of fruitflies and nematode worms, while 223 human genes originated in bacteria.[2] And, as Charles Lewis points out in his book *Green Nature/ Human Nature*, haemoglobin, the critical factor in our blood, is only slightly different chemically from chlorophyll, the "lifeblood" of plants. Indeed, certain aspects of basic metabolism are remarkably similar in plants and animals (including humans).[3]

We may be just a small part of the overall picture of nature, but we have a totally disproportionate impact on it. Through an exaggerated and misguided sense of control, we have, in an astonishingly short time, devastated ecosystems, transformed an estimated 10 per cent of the earth's surface from forest or range-land into desert, ravaged water supplies and polluted the atmosphere—all huge problems defying easy solution. But as we focus more and more on setting right our own small worlds, the cumulative effect just might help to tip the scales in the earth's and our favor.

Our connections with nature are as deeply rooted in our psyches and spirits as they are in our bodies. Noted Harvard biologist E.O. Wilson calls this innate connection "biophilia"—a natural affinity for life that is the very essence of our humanity and that binds us to all other living species. "Our existence depends on [it], our spirit is woven from it, hope rises on its currents."[4] Our attraction to and fascination with nature harks back to our Stone-Age ancestors, hunter-gatherers for whom "the smell of water, the hum of a bee, the directional bend of a plant stalk mattered...." It was a matter of survival. "The brain appears to have kept its

old capacities, its channeled quickness. We stay alert and alive in the vanished forests of the world."[5] Tending our gardens, or walking through a park, we are connecting with ancient memories and finding tranquility and harmony.

Psychologists Stephen and Rachel Kaplan have researched the restorative effects of nature— how it relieves mental fatigue and how the dreamily distracted state we so easily fall into outdoors actually refreshes our ability to concentrate. (I have yet to get from the front garden to the garage to retrieve a tool in one uninterrupted trip; I always stop to watch a butterfly probe for nectar, or marvel at those bulbs I'd totally forgotten I had planted.) The Kaplans conclude that, "Nature is not just 'nice'… it is a vital ingredient in healthy human functioning."[6]

In addition, researchers such as Roger S. Ulrich of Texas A&M and Mary Honeyman of University of Illinois have found that simply looking at greenery can reduce stress, lower blood pressure, decrease muscle tension and increase positive feelings. Ulrich studied patients in hospital recovering from gall bladder surgery and discovered that those with a view of vegetation had shorter stays,

It may seem odd, but getting distracted, by the sight of tiny snowdrops for example, is actually part of a restorative process that refreshes the ability to concentrate.

required less medication and were easier to deal with than those looking at brick walls. Cancer patients who gardened regained their normal lives faster than those who did not. Prisoners who overlooked trees and gardens had fewer medical problems and symptoms of stress.[7]

The compelling impact of specifically designed therapeutic gardens in healthcare settings is being recognized. A 1992 study in British Columbia found that, after a special garden was installed at a residence for Alzheimer's patients, the number of violent incidents declined 19 per cent over two years.[8] And these gardens aren't just for the patients. Cooper Marcus' and Barnes' survey of 24 California hospitals revealed that the most frequent users of the gardens were staff seeking respite from high-stress work situations. One employee summed it up bluntly, saying, "I'll tell you this...if it weren't for the garden, we'd all be on Prozac!"[9]

In Australia, researchers studied the value home gardeners placed on their gardens and concluded that gardens "have the potential to satisfy nine basic human needs (subsistence, protection, affection, understanding, participation, leisure, creation, identity and freedom) across four existential states (being, having, doing and interacting).[11] Somehow, I don't think stamp collecting comes close.

More difficult to measure is the aesthetic pleasure we derive from nature—that take-your-breath-away beauty it tosses out so wantonly. But when a group of British children aged 12 to 14 were asked to list the seven things they found most beautiful, the responses were almost always natural objects.[12] Only later do we assign beauty to things such as sculpture and paintings (and what do many of those depict, but nature?).

The power of plants extends beyond the individual. Greener communities mean healthier surroundings through climate and pollution modification, healthier inhabitants through homegrown organic vegetables, greater social contact and cooperation, improved property values, lower incidences of crime, better business activity and a sense of civic pride, not to mention the considerable benefits to the environment and the creatures with whom we co-habit. (See Chapter 11 for more on urban greening.)

Sadly, environmental degradation and our estrangement from nature are not new. Primal peoples, Greeks, Egyptians, Hindus and Taoists saw "the cosmos as an organism which is sentient, rational, pervaded by harmony, and of which human beings are parts reflecting the nature of the whole"[13] —what historian J. Donald Hughes of the University of Denver calls "ecological consciousness." But with environmental degradation (the ancient Mesopotamians did themselves in by deforesting their mountainsides) came a psychological split. Reverence for life disappeared and nature was cast as wild, chaotic, something to be subjugated and plundered. Today, Hughes feels that the weight of environmental threats such as loss of the ozone layer, global warming and the extinction of thousands of species "have made it impossible to take a stable, supportive world for granted."[14] Restoration of the environment then is essential to psychic health (after all, how perverse would it be for psychologists to focus on helping people to adjust and be happy in such a world?). We need a new ecological consciousness. H.L. Leff describes it as having a sense of self as a part of a larger holistic system; an understanding and awareness of the ecological processes within this system; a high ability to enjoy and appreciate things in themselves (not just for their usefulness to people); a life-affirming value system and a cooperative orientation toward people and other living things.[15] Recognizing that a deep relationship to nature is a healing factor for the psyche, Hughes suggests "eco-therapy." I call it gardening.

Horticultural Therapy

Nature has long been our sanctuary and intimate healer, since ancient Egyptians prescribed walks in the garden for the mentally disturbed. In 1985, researchers asked 300 people to visualize "an environment that would be healing" for someone feeling helpless, wounded or in pain. Every single person described an environment with nature.[10] Confirmed now by science as well as anecdote, this healing power (which we can all find in our gardens) underlies the concept of horticultural therapy.

Defined in North America in the 1970s as a therapeutic tool, horticultural therapy uses nature and gardening activities to improve body, mind and spirit with the intervention of a trained horticultural therapist. Settings range from hospitals and nursing homes to hospices and prisons. Interestingly, horticultural therapy is growing particularly popular for those with illnesses such as AIDS, Alzheimer's and cancer—diseases for which medicine doesn't have the "magic bullet." There may be no cure, but there certainly is room for healing.

Eminently adaptable, horticultural therapy can range from a few pots on a windowsill to acres of gardens and can involve everything from starting seeds and pressing flowers to water-gardening and growing prize tomatoes. At the geriatric center where I assist in horticultural therapy programs, we are lucky to have a large greenhouse as well as a roof garden, and I can vouch for the fact that far more grows in the garden than just plants: self-esteem, optimism, camaraderie, creativity, satisfaction, a sense of purpose, as well as physical and mental abilities.

Natural Archetypes

Nature covers a lot of ground: Are some types of landscape more healing than others? What kinds of landscape do we prefer and why? Wilson makes the fascinating assertion that humans make habitat choices based on certain key features of the ancient habitat: the African savanna, a "vast parklike grassland dotted by groves and scattered trees."[16] After thousands of years, despite the varied geography we find ourselves in, he says we still work to re-create this archetypal environment or "proto-paysage" "in such improbable sites as formal gardens, cemeteries and suburban shopping malls, hungering for open spaces but not a barren landscape."[17]

Scientist Gordon Orians cites three key features of this ancient environment: the savanna itself, a higher point of land (cliff, ridge or hill) serving as both shelter and vantage point, and bodies of water: "It seems that whenever people are given a free choice, they move to open tree-studded land on prominences overlooking water. This worldwide tendency is no longer dictated by the hard necessities of hunter-gatherer life. It has become largely aesthetic, a spur to art and landscaping. Those who exercise the greatest degree of free choice, the rich and powerful, congregate on high land above lakes and rivers and along ocean bluffs. On such sites they build palaces, villas, temples and corporate retreats."[18] Ancient Roman or contemporary suburbanite, we have made and continue to make gardens featuring carefully placed trees, rolling lawns, ponds and waterfalls, along with sheltering gazebos, follies and arbors from which to survey our domains. In fact, tree-studded expanses of grass are so ubiquitous, they threaten to distort our sense of what natural really means. (See Chapter 5 for more on this.)

Then there are those who believe that in addition to these ancient impulses we are always trying to re-create the environment in which we grew up. Landscape architect Topher Delaney, designer of many healing gardens, says she always asks new clients where they spent their first six years, because that will tell her what kind of garden they are really seeking. Julie Moir Messervy, author of *The Inward Garden*, calls them spatial memories—memories of the favorite places of our lives, especially childhood, which we can draw on to create more fulfilling, satisfying spaces. By thinking about what types of places have given us the most positive feelings in the past, we can invest our gardens with greater personal significance and healing possibilities.

There has been much discussion about healing gardens in all kinds of settings, and there are some common threads regarding what makes a garden a healing space. But just as no pill cures all ailments, there is no single prescription for a healing

Spatial Archetypes

As author Julie Moir Messervy points out, spatial archetypes can be seen or translated in every garden.

- the sea, or immersion (being in a glade surrounded by the forest, for example)
- the cave, protected yet with a view out (the garden house or gazebo)
- the harbor, safety but with a wider view (a bench set against a hedge or wall)
- the island, isolated in a different world (a terrace surrounded by a lush planting)
- the promontory, or that cliff as vantage point (a tiered garden, a deck projecting over a ravine)
- the mountain, from which we can see everything (a tower or, more symbolically, a tall statue or obelisk)
- the sky, signaling transcendence (framing it in hedges, trees, or reflecting it in ponds or mirrors).[19]

garden. If you hate the color orange, then there's absolutely no point putting orange in your garden, no matter what its supposed benefit. If you work at a computer all day, chances are you won't want to stand and stare at a solitary *objet* in a monochromatic space, no matter how artfully composed. Each person's needs are unique—the marvelous thing about gardens and nature is that they can fill every single one. The more meaning the garden has for you, the more individual it is—the more you bring your spirit and intellect and heart to bear on it—the greater the rewards.

Some Elements of Healing Garden Design

Where to begin the creation of your personal garden sanctuary? Leave aside questions of roses red or delphiniums blue for the moment and consider these design elements which are common to healing gardens of all kinds. Once you are assured of these main ingredients, you can add color, style and form, spicing the mix to taste.

An Inviting Entry A decorative gate or opening in the hedgerow, or simply pots with climbing vines will mark a threshold, offer an intriguing peek into the garden and give a sense of moving into another world.

Diverse and Interesting Sensual Stimulation (known as the kid-in-a-candy-store effect) In gardens, the more abundant and complex the natural setting, as long as it is perceived as harmonious and coherent, the more powerful the psychological benefit for stress relief and restoration.[20] The more elaborate the garden, the more there is to derive pleasure from, and the richer it is for all its inhabitants—flora and fauna alike.

In chapters to come I will talk about biodiversity and how critical it is to healthy ecosystems, as well as explore the diverse charms of the sensory garden.

Enclosure Enclosed spaces provide security and a sense of sanctuary that encourages reflection and self-renewal. The entire garden may be enclosed or just a personal haven within it. The enclosure can range from a seat in a vine-covered arbor to a thriving "edge" full of plants and critters. (See Chapter 5.)

A healing space needs enclosure for a sense of security and privacy; this patio garden with its rhythmic fence, sheltering overhead beams and harmonious combination of wood, stone and greenery provides both.

A Sense of Mystery A garden should beguile. It may have a path going off into the distance, a glimpse of a structure through the trees, or the sound of water—something that draws you in, stimulates and involves you in the garden. Never underestimate the power of pleasurable surprise.

Natural Forms We are comforted by familiar forms that hold all sorts of symbolic meanings. One of the most potent is the circle—the circle of life, the sun, the moon, the earth, the container of yin and yang. The natural shapes of hills, trees and ponds are deeply pleasing in a way that hard-edged human constructions are not. Topiaries are fun, but most plants are happier left to their natural devices (the world definitely doesn't need more forsythia "balls").

Water holding the sky, plants the greenest of greens—these elements are at the heart of healing places.

Light and Dark There should be a variety of spaces that offer different combinations of sun, shade and shelter from wind. Such diversity creates a private world that responds to different moods, and an array of "mini-worlds" or microclimates that will sustain a number of richly populated plant communities.

Places for One or More Than One Ideally, the garden should have room for you to retreat in solitude or to be social, with a comfy seat, whichever your preference.

Water and Lush, Healthy Plantings Thriving plants (grown organically, needless to say), bathed in light, with a pond close by—these are the stuff upon which our lives depend, and when those elements appear in balance, it's a harmony we recognize and respond to deep within our psyches. The garden is not an escape *from* reality; it's an escape *to* reality.

Synergy and Biodiversity

A couple of words that recur in this book are *synergy* and *biodiversity*. Every corporate merger these days is heralded as "a new synergy," be it print and television, hardware and software, or widgets and gadgets. But synergy (from the Greek *synergos* meaning working together) is a fundamental aspect of the natural world. It is usually taken to mean "the whole is greater than the sum of its parts" but a more accurate definition is "the whole produces a different effect from what the parts produce on their own." Dr. Peter A. Corning writes, "…many parts may be needed to make a whole, yet the loss of even a single part may be sufficient to destroy it. (We refer to this methodology as 'synergy minus one.')…. Imagine what would happen if…the Transfer RNA were removed from the machinery of reproduction, or the beak from one of Darwin's finches, or the vowels from the words in [this paragraph]…or the wheel from an automobile." He adds that removing one element doesn't necessarily mean immediate catastrophe (one herring flunking out of a school of herrings will not seriously endanger the rest), but even small losses or changes can ultimately affect the total.[21]

One scientist will declare that all life depends on the soil, another that all life depends on water. Others tout our dependence on bacteria, air, photosynthesis and so on. All life depends on all these things—together. They are inextricably entwined. Take one away—or damage it irreparably—and the whole system collapses. Every system in nature is synergistic. Take soil for example: organic matter is great stuff but plants struggle if grown in organic matter alone; growing them in water (hydroponic) is fine in the short term but not in the long term (they don't reproduce well); it takes a balanced mixture of organic matter, minerals, air and water to create the ideal growing medium.

It's astounding to think that plants are made up of just 20 basic elements (carbon, oxygen, nitrogen, etc.). These are combined into molecules, which are combined into cells, which form tissues, which form organs, which form the total plant. And in all those combinations, most plants are still 90 per cent water, yet look at the miraculous variety, the infinite spins nature puts on the remaining 10 per cent! Call it synergy in spades. Every component part contributes to the life activity; remove one and cells start to die. "From air, water and the dust of the earth, atoms unite, albeit temporarily, into living, functioning plants and animals. And when, inevitably, the spark of life is lost, it is back to those primal forms that the elements return."[22]

That wondrous variety is what is meant by biodiversity. And it is critical to maintaining the health of every plant, animal and ecosystem on earth. Since every system is synergistic, then the loss of even one element will have an effect. Multiple losses can be devastating. Loss of biodiversity is so far-reaching it constitutes the greatest threat to the health of the planet and its inhabitants. Of course, the earth's ecosystems have been evolving for millions of years, recovering from sometimes catastrophic changes, and they will continue to do so in ways we cannot imagine, with or without us. But it behooves us to remember our place in this ecosphere and to do everything in our power to understand and preserve its complex systems. Left to their own devices, ecosystems naturally evolve and grow more diverse and stable—and what is the ultimate state of the most biodiverse, stable ecosystems? Harmony—rather dryly described as a "proportionate, orderly, co-operative condition"[23]—but the state that we instinctively recognize as being set right.

Hidden Harmonies

Nature's shapes and forms carry a weight of human symbolism, but possess their own magic, too.

Circles, Spheres and Spirals

Among the most powerful is the circle. One crisp, sunny day in Winnipeg, I visited Oodena: The Celebration Circle at the confluence of the Red and Assiniboine rivers. The moment I passed between two of the 17 sandstone pillars surrounding this large open circle, I felt a tangible change in the air, the energy, whatever you want to call it. It was so striking I walked out and back in, and experienced the same thing. There was nothing mechanical there, simply stone and plants, wind and sunshine, and something quite ineffable.

The circle embodies unity, completeness, equality; it is the circle of life, of the seasons, of the earth, moon and sun. It's a universal symbol, from England's megalithic Stonehenge to India's mandalas and native Americans' medicine wheels. These last, which are circles with "spokes," are made up of 36 stones, each with a different meaning, each a tool to increase understanding of our ties to the earth. There are four parts: a center circle, the moons and totems, the spirit keepers and the spirit paths.[24] As the wheel implies, it is not static, it is a journey you take, moving to different positions in the wheel, learning and growing at all levels of being. One of the best known medicine wheels is on Medicine

Mountain in Wyoming. Eighty-one feet (25 meters) in diameter, with 28 "spokes" (roughly corresponding to the lunar cycle), it is thought to have had astronomical as well as ceremonial purposes.

The more intently we observe nature, the more patterns emerge in endless variations on a theme. Circles (and spheres) are omnipresent, as is the spiral, symbol of growth, evolution and the continuity of life. Spirals are echoed in a snail's shell, an emerging fiddlehead, and a sunflower's seed arrangement (an artfully efficient way of packing as many seeds as possible into the space).

Fibonacci Numbers

Leonardo Pisano Fibonacci (1175–1250) was a mathematician who set out a fascinating numerical sequence. Simply put, each number is the sum of the previous two: thus, 1, 1, 2, 3, 5, 8, 13, 21, 34, 55, 89, 144…. What's fascinating is that these

Symbol of evolution and the continuity of life, the spiral, here limned in flower petals, is found everywhere in nature, from a snail's shell to a sunflower's seed arrangement.

numbers abound in nature. For example, the base of a pine cone may have 13 clockwise spirals and eight counterclockwise spirals. The leaves on trees are staggered around the stem to gather the most light and water. In most trees, these leaf arrangements are Fibonacci numbers. For example, on a beech or hazel, we have one clockwise rotation before meeting a leaf positioned directly above the first, passing three leaves on the way (expressed as 1/3), while poplar and pear require three rotations, passing eight leaves on the way (or 3/8). The number of flower petals and sunflower seed spirals also display the Fibonacci series.

Golden Ratio and Full Spectrum Harmonic Sound

The golden ratio or golden mean is expressed as 1.618. It is unique in that the ratio of the whole to the larger portion is the same as the ratio of the larger portion to the smaller portion. This aesthetically pleasing proportion appears in everything from the ancient pyramids to Leonardo da Vinci's "Last Supper." Artists and architects have long known that using it in their work enhances the sense of beauty, balance and harmony. But nature was there first. The golden ratio can be found in practically every natural element from flowers to leaves to cactus to a butterfly's wing. So it's no surprise to me that in a garden surrounded by a zillion examples of the golden mean, we should be infused with beauty, balance and harmony. (A further intriguing fact: the ratios of the Fibonacci numbers to each other all come very close to the golden mean.)

I'm certain we intuit this proportion without being aware of it. For example, when you're planting and set the pots out in a grouping and step back to look at it—why does it look wrong, until you adjust this one just so and that one a bit there, and then you step back, and suddenly it looks "right"? If you measured, it's very likely you would find it had clicked into the golden proportion.

Ross Barrable, maker of wind harps (see Chapter 10 for more about his work), points out that the overtones generated by full spectrum harmonic sound (such as ocean waves and wind) exhibit the same golden ratio, adding even greater resonance to nature's boundless harmony.

The Labyrinth

Symbols and silence come together in the spiritual path known as the labyrinth. An ancient meditative tool, a labyrinth is usually three, seven or eleven concentric circles and represents a journey into our own center and back out again into the world. It can be set as a pattern into a paved area (as was done at the California Pacific Medical Center in San Francisco), formed with stones or simply sculpted out of grass. Unlike a maze, which is a puzzle with twists and turns and dead ends, a labyrinth has just one meandering but purposeful path inwards, which you retrace on your return journey of self-discovery.

Whatever form it takes, the healing garden affords us the opportunity to gaze inward and outward in an intimate communion that renews us physically, emotionally and psychologically. By gaining a deeper understanding of nature's infinitely wondrous workings, we can draw on that healing power to restore balance and harmony in ourselves and to the earth.

2

A SENSE OF HUMUS

More organization and complexity exist in a handful of soil than on the surfaces of all the other planets combined.

EDWARD O. WILSON,
IN SEARCH OF NATURE, 1996

To plunge your hands into the soil is to grasp the heart of the matter. Grab a handful, feel its texture like nothing else in the world, smell that earthy sweetness, peer at it closely…. If you're lucky, you'll see bits of leaves and even twigs, some grit or chunks of clay, a tracery of fine plant roots, a host of tiny USOs (unidentified soil organisms) and an indignant earthworm or three. The rest is mysterious brown stuff that crumbles like so much chocolate cake. (If, on the other hand, your soil is thin, powdery stuff that runs through your fingers like sand in an hourglass or has the unremitting feel of dried-out plasticine, you have work to do.)

Soil nourishes directly or indirectly every living thing on earth. Soil controls the chemistry of air and water. Soil is where it all begins—and ends. So just what is soil? William Bryant Logan calls it stardust since all the elements originated as cosmic dust.[1] More prosaically, it's usually described as a combination of minerals, organic matter, air and water. But that utterly ignores the vital fact that soil is swarming with millions of microorganisms such as bacteria, fungi, algae and nematodes. It's so rich in diversity it has been called an underground rain forest—but the amount we really know about these denizens of the dirt is like the tip of an iceberg.

It's easy to forget that the seemingly solid ground we tread on is, in fact, a living thing. The skin of the earth, soil is constantly moving and changing, responding to winds, human abuse, chemicals, floods, drought and varying temperatures. And it is surprisingly fragile. It can take 2,000 years for nature to create one inch (2.5 cm) of topsoil, yet it can be destroyed in a (relative) flash. In *Gardening for the Future of the Earth,* Shapiro and Harrisson tell us "an average of 39 tons (35.4 metric tons) of soil is lost per acre of farmed land in the United States every year." How? Because the "massive input of fertilizers and pesticides destroys the natural balance and ecosystem of the soil."[2] Repeated tilling also kills many soil-dwellers and breaks down the natural soil structure, leaving it more susceptible to erosion by wind and water. Similarly, when all the trees are removed and grasslands are overgrazed, the surface no longer absorbs the rain, the water table shrinks lower and the soil is sucked dry. Dryness plus lack of life equals desert—the ultimate result. Despite the rich forests in Southern Ontario, by the late 1800s, after much landclearing, farming and tilling, three deserts were actually forming there. Only determined tree-planting programs halted the process. As recently as 1997, the U.S. Department of the Interior reported that a staggering 37 per cent of the country is significantly susceptible to desertification.[3]

Soil: More than Meets the Eye

A minuscule amount of soil (.03 ounces/one gram) can contain 5 billion bacteria. Around the roots of a healthy plant (the *rhizosphere*), there could be 200 billion bacteria. These microscopic, one-celled creatures are both good guys and bad guys. Most perform such valuable functions as fixing nitrogen, i.e., converting nitrogen from the air to nitrates and breaking down organic matter. A sub-category called *actinomycetes* secrete antibiotics as a weapon against competing microbes, and this is where we get such valuable antibiotics as streptomycin, erythromycin and the tetracyclines.

In fact, bacteria are used in a wealth of vaccines, medical enzymes and foods (yogurt wouldn't be yogurt without lactic acid bacteria). For better or for worse, the genetic systems of bacteria are the foundation of the biotechnology industry. For example, "super strains" of bacteria have been genetically engineered to degrade petroleum products and can be a valuable tool in cleaning up oil spills. More controversially, they're used to introduce genes into plants to make them more pest- or disease-resistant. (See Chapter 8 for more on this.)

In the rhizosphere, a special kind of fungi called *mycorrhizae* actually penetrate the roots. The fungi send out long strands of feeding structures called *hyphae*, which draw nutrients for the plant well beyond its root-reach; in return, the plant feeds the fungi. This symbiotic relationship is incredibly beneficial— in fact, you can now buy mycorrhizae inoculants. (If you have several of the same kind of plant and see that one is declining while the others thrive, try scooping up some soil and a few tiny roots from a healthy one and "inoculating" the sick one; it could do the trick, especially since mycorrhizae tend to be plant-specific.)

Also playing their roles in the cast of millions are algae, which take up carbon dioxide from the air and convert it to oxygen; nematodes (tiny worms, some good and some bad); and simple-celled amoebae and protozoa. Bigger in size, if not in importance, are the

Ways to Kill Your Soil

Compact it.
Roll heavy equipment or tromp about on your soil, especially when it's wet. Particularly effective for clay soils which will soon resemble concrete.

Douse it with pesticides.
Attempt to eliminate every sort of undesirable critter or fungus by indiscriminate spraying with a chemical arsenal. This is guaranteed to kill all the beneficial creatures that make the soil fertile and productive. Another side effect is the pollution of the groundwater.

Overfeed with chemical fertilizers.
Get bigger, fatter plants immediately, but starve the microorganisms and send those earthworms packing.

Never mulch.
Sweep every leaf and twig off the ground and discard them, but keep trying to grow things so any remaining nutrients in the soil will be depleted even more rapidly.

For every living thing, soil is where it all begins—and ends.

beetles, centipedes, mites, spiders, snails, wood lice, ants and worms. The life of the soil depends on all these creatures feeding on plants, nutrients and each other, transforming organic matter, excreting and, ultimately, dying.

Without all these decomposers, we'd have trouble keeping our heads above the piles of debris. If it weren't for all that munching, there would be leaf litter 60 feet (18 m) deep in a 2,000-year-old forest, instead of a constant four inches (10 cm) or so.[4] The leaves and twigs, the remnants of understory plants and the remains of animals and insects are all returned to the soil to nourish the next generation.

Interestingly, forest soils, especially coniferous forests, are fungi-dominated, while grassland soils are bacteria-dominated. Our gardens are generally in between and fairly balanced. But if for some reason, forest soils become bacteria-dominated, they will adversely affect the trees growing there and, in the case of conifers, prevent seedlings from growing. Understanding this relationship underlines why we should group plants together as they grow in nature. It also means that if you have a grassy meadow and plan to turn it into woodland or vice versa, you need to substantially alter the soil to have any chance of success.

Soil minerals, born of rock and ground down by the action of wind, water and weather over thousands of years, come in different particle sizes. Although thousands of different soils have been classified by scientists (with mouthful names such as *orthic melanic brunisolic* and *brown solodized solonetzic*), they share the basic ingredients. The smallest particles are clay (less than .00008 inch/.002 mm diameter), the largest sand (from .002 inch/.06 mm to .08 inch/2 mm) and in between are silt (from .0008 inch/.002 mm to .002 inch/.06 mm). All are present in most soils but the dominant one determines the kind of soil. You can feel the difference: clay soil is smooth and sticky in your fingers, like plasticine. Silty soil feels silky or soapy, while a sandy soil is gritty.

Clay soils are dense, heavy and hold water (and nutrients) extremely well. But they are easily waterlogged, hard for roots to penetrate and tough to dig in. (The wet clay soil of North American prairies isn't called "gumbo" for nothing.) If you have heavy clay soil and are planting a relatively small area, save yourself major grief—take out the clay to a depth of 18 to 24 inches (45 to 60 cm) and replace it with triple mix. Even Sisyphus would prefer his rock to trying to amend really heavy clay.

Sandy soils are loose, easy to work and well-draining (the plus side) but (the down side) water tends to run through before plant roots can capture vital nutrients. Areas around lakes were often once lake bottoms. Near Lake Ontario, where I live, as in many areas near the Great Lakes, I have only to dig down a foot (30 cm) and there is golden, which-way-to-the-beach sand. Silty soils are in between but are thin in nutrients and water retention.

Humus

Clay/sand/silt determine the texture of the soil. The more critical element is the structure: that porous "crumbly-ness" characteristic of the dream soil known as loam. Fully half of loam is air and water, with 5 or 6 per cent organic matter, and a mix of sand, silt and slightly less clay. But that doesn't explain the spongy, sweet-smelling, devil's-food-cake quality that makes gardeners salivate. The magic ingredient is humus—created as masses of microorganisms work their chemical alchemy on decomposed organic matter.

Its sponginess is the secret: just as important as the soil particles are the spaces between them (like any good skin, the secret is in the pores). They hold air and water, which really isn't water any more but a soil "plasma" full of nutrients for tiny questing roots. Thriving plants send out more roots, loosening the soil and pulling up nutrients from below. Fallen leaves and roots that die (root systems are constantly being replaced) add more organic matter for the microorganisms, and the synergy just keeps on rolling. Petrik calls stable humus "the connector of life"[5]—where everything that dies returns to decompose and feed new life. The process of making humus, like photosynthesis, cannot be synthetically duplicated. We can only supply the ingredients and let nature "bake" the cake.

What Is pH?

The relative acidity or alkalinity of your soil is expressed as a pH level (the ratio of hydrogen to hydroxyl ions in the soil water). When they are equal, it is neutral (pH7). A higher number means alkaline; lower is acid. You should care about these numbers because plants take up the most nutrients in the middle pH range. There are ways of moderating the pH of your soil (adding lime to acid soils; sulfur and pine needles to alkaline), but it's difficult to make big changes on a large scale. If you have alkaline soil and you desperately want to grow acid-lovers such as rhododendrons, put them in a pot where you can control the growing medium. Otherwise, simply choose plants partial to your conditions. Plus, if you add plenty of organic matter, and have healthy, well-aerated soil that's alive with earthworms and all those good micro-guys, the pH factor is not nearly as critical.

Dirt Tidbits

When you spade down into your soil, you will likely see a sandwich of different colored layers: the top (usually the darkest brown) is organic matter, the next layer down is topsoil. Then comes the subsoil and finally the parent material or weathered rock. These layers are called *horizons* and should be disturbed as little as possible. (See Chapter 8 for more about digging and tilling.)

Perfect soil is as rare as black tulips. The best thing you can do to "grow" soil is add organic matter, which can be chopped leaves, hay, grass clippings, bark chips, potato peelings, coffee grounds or yesterday's newspaper, as mulch or compost. (See Chapter 7 for the dirt on composting.)

In healthy soil, the good guys outnumber the bad, and researchers are finding that correctly balanced soils are indeed disease-suppressing. They also find that vegetables grown with chemical fertilizers contain fewer nutrients than those grown in the humus-rich soil described above. Synthetic fertilizers destroy microorganisms, upset the soil's chemical balance and encourage leaching of essential minerals.

Leave your leaves in place—it's one of the easiest and best ways to "grow" soil.

Mulch Marvelous Mulch

If the three most important things in real estate are location, location, location, then gardening's big three are mulch, mulch, mulch. If you do nothing else in the garden, mulch. In fact, if you mulch, you won't have as much to do.

Top 10 Reasons to Mulch

Mulch is a material applied to the surface of the soil that:

1. Helps the soil absorb water by keeping the soil surface loose and open.
2. Keeps weeds down.
3. Regulates the temperature of the soil, keeping it cool in summer and reducing risk of root damage in winter.
4. Conserves moisture in the soil by reducing evaporation.
5. Prevents erosion by wind and water.
6. Keeps soil from splashing up onto foliage, which could lead to bacterial or fungal disease.
7. Holds fruit and vegetables off the ground keeping them free of soil rot.
8. Reduces soil compaction from heavy rain or foot traffic.
9. Adds organic matter to the soil as the lower layer of mulch decomposes.
10. Reduces need for digging/tilling because earthworms thrive in well-mulched organic soil.

Bonus: Mulch looks attractive.

I can't think of another process in the garden that does as much in one fell swoop. Not surprising, really, when all we're doing is mimicking what nature does on its own. Apply mulch to a depth of two inches (5 cm), for fairly fine material, to four inches (10 cm), for coarser mulches, over the entire root zone of the plant. Winter mulch should be applied after the ground is frozen which isn't always easy. If you mulch only once, do it in spring and keep it topped up over summer. Keep mulch a few inches away from the trunks of woody plants and the crowns of perennials since trapped moisture can cause disease problems. Mulch also provides a home for all kinds of critters, but I figure there are as many good guys as bad in there. Still, if you think your mulch is harboring too many slugs, say, switch to a different, less hospitable material.

Eating Dirt

Small children seem to put everything in their mouths and, according to an EPA study, they ingest .007 ounces (200 milligrams) of soil a day. But this is a concern only if the soil is contaminated by heavy metals or chemical residue from pesticides and fertilizers. Over a lifetime, between soil and dust, we take in an average of just under .0007 ounces (20 milligrams) a day (which works out to 1.08 pounds/.48 kg)! Deliberate soil-eating, regarded as a disorder called *pica*, has been practiced in various cultures around the world, usually by pregnant women, who eat clay. It's thought that minerals in the clay offset dietary deficiencies and help morning sickness.

Then again, Madagascar's golden bamboo lemurs may be on to something. Every day, these 3.3 pound (1.5 kg) creatures munch enough cyanide-laden giant bamboo shoots and leaves to kill a human being. But they regularly clamber down to nibble on soil, which scientists believe could contain antidotes to their lethal lunch. Soil not only nourishes the foods we eat and the plants we enjoy, but it may literally heal us. It holds more mysteries than we could, at first glance, ever imagine.

Mulch Menu

There are plenty of mulches to choose from, including:

Bark
Available in little chips, big chunks and shredded. Durable and attractive, good for shrub plantings, but may be too coarse for perennial beds.

Cocoa shells
Attractive dark brown color and a chocolatey aroma when first applied. Occasionally harbor mold so don't apply deeper than two inches (5 cm).

Compost
A great mulch, soil amendment and fertilizer. Its only drawback as a mulch is that weed seeds landing in it think they've died and gone to heaven, and grow with unimaginable zeal.

Grass clippings
High nitrogen and water content means fresh clippings should be applied thinly. A thick layer will mat and get stinky due to anaerobic decomposition (rotting *sans* oxygen).

Leaves
A top-notch mulch and usually readily available. Best chopped so they don't mat. We shred our leaves with the lawn mower, let them compost over winter and, come spring, mix them with well-rotted manure for a terrific mulch.

Hay/straw
Excellent for vegetable gardens and as a winter mulch.

Newspaper
Shredding, as is often advised, is too much like work. Whole sheets are best used as an underlayment with another mulch on top for shrub borders and pathways. Also effective in a very thick layer (with mulch on top) at smothering grass and weeds prior to creating a new planting bed.

Peat moss
Do *not* use this as a mulch unless you live in constant rain. It dries out easily, forming an impermeable crust and is wretchedly difficult to remoisten. It can be used wet as a soil amendment for

Straw makes an excellent mulch for vegetable gardens and can also provide good winter insulation.

Use whatever natural material is available for mulch; here pine cones are effective; I use the flowers, nuts and leaves from my beech tree as mulch in my garden.

acid-loving plants, but pine needles and oak leaves do the same and aren't a non-renewable (at least in our lifetimes) resource.

Pine needles and cones
Lightweight, water permeable and long lasting. A bit prickly to work with.

Polyethylene film/landscape fabric
These are inorganic sheet mulches, used primarily on vegetable beds. Plants are placed through slits in the film or fabric. Landscape fabric, also used under stone paths or dry stream beds to keep weeds down, will degrade in sunlight so requires another covering on top. The film may be black or clear, and makes for warmer soil.

Sea shells
Sharp edges deter slugs; light color reflects heat onto plants.

Worms: Your Garden's Unsung Heroes

You know your soil is healthy if you have earthworms, which Aristotle described as "the intestines of the earth." These deceptively simple little critters will do a huge amount of work for you if you let them. Soil movers and processors par excellence, they are amazingly strong, easily pushing aside stones 60 times their weight. Their tunneling loosens the soil, allowing air and moisture to reach the plants' roots and helping the bacteria to do their thing. As they work, the worms ingest the soil and any organic material they come across. They also pull in organic matter from the soil surface—when you see little bunches of leaf stems sticking up, you know the worms are busy on the other end pulling the leaves into their burrows.

What goes in must come out, and worms leave castings that are rich in organic matter and nutrients including nitrogen, phosphorus, potassium—in other words, free, all-natural fertilizer, delivered right to where it's needed. A good, humus-rich soil could have 25 worms per cubic foot which translates into more than eight pounds (3.6 kg) of superior fertilizer over the gardening year. Earthworms also produce calcium carbonate which helps to moderate the soil's pH balance, acid or alkaline. You may not fancy earthworms as a snack (though there are people in the world who do), but they are 82 per cent protein and apparently reduce cholesterol levels. Maybe those robins are smarter than we think.

Tetanus Prevention

- Wear gloves, especially if you have any sort of cut or abrasion.
- Handle sharp tools carefully.
- Should you get a deep penetrating wound anywhere on your body while gardening:
  - Thoroughly cleanse it with soap and water, and
  - If you haven't had a tetanus booster shot in the past five years, get one. (Current recommendations call for tetanus boosters every 10 years. If you suffer a deep, penetrating wound and haven't had a tetanus booster shot in the past five years, get one.)

Tetanus and Thorn Alert

Soil is home to some of the most deadly bacteria including those responsible for tuberculosis, anthrax, leprosy and cholera. One of the most serious for the home gardener is *Clostridium tetani*, an anaerobic bacillus that causes *tetanus*, a serious infectious disease of the nervous system. Also called *lockjaw*, it produces involuntary muscle spasms, particularly of the jaw muscles. These bacteria are widely present in garden soil, especially cultivated soils. If they get into a deep wound, they flourish, producing toxins that enter the bloodstream, are picked up by nerves and carried to the spine. Once tetanus has spread, the mortality rate is 60 per cent.[6]

And watch those rose thorns. Pricks from them can provide entry for a fungus, *Sporothrix schenckii*, which causes a disease called *sporotrichosis*. It usually affects the skin and initially is a little reddish bump like an insect bite, usually within three weeks of exposure. Additional bumps like boils appear and take a long time to heal. Very rarely, it infects the joints, lungs and central nervous system, but can be treated with a drug called *itraconazole*.

The fungus is found in other thorny plants, too, as well as sphagnum moss and hay. According to medical reports, outbreaks have occurred in nursery workers who handled sphagnum moss topiaries, children playing on baled hay and greenhouse workers handling bayberry thorns.[7] While sporotrichosis isn't that common, it makes sense for the home gardener, especially anyone who has a weakened immune system, to wear gloves when handling these materials.

Still, there are times, especially in late spring when everything is burgeoning, that the urge to feel the warmth of the soil on your skin is irresistible. For in that touch you can sense the green promise held in soil's deep dark mysteries and realize its part in the miraculous alchemy of air, dust and water.

3

WATER WAYS

Water is a symbol of grace....
In many cultures, water appears
as a reflection or an image of the soul.

CHRISTOPHER L. C. E. WITCOMBE,
SACRED PLACES

Our bodies are 70 per cent water. Most plants are 90 per cent water, and more than half of the world's plant and animal species live in the water. People need two quarts (2 L) of water a day and can go only a few days without it—and they are totally dependent on exterior means to make that water drinkable. That's where plants are superior. Many have sophisticated mechanisms to survive long periods of drought, or they have adapted to arid conditions. In the arctic tundra, plants grow and bloom at time-lapse speed in the brief summer, then retreat into the safety of dormancy. Cacti and succulents store water in their plump, fleshy leaves. Plants such as lamb's ears (*Stachys*) have silvery leaves that, close inspection reveals, are covered with a fine fuzz. The pale color deflects the sun's rays, while the little hairs act as moisture retainers. Others such as rosemary (*Rosmarinus*) have narrow, leathery leaves almost like needles, exposing as little leaf surface to drying air as possible.

Though we all know that water is two molecules of hydrogen and one molecule of oxygen (H_2O), and scientists have explored the amazing properties of this substance that can exist as a gas, a solid and a liquid, we still don't understand exactly how and why water acts as it does.

What is certain is that water is the universal solvent: without it, neither plants nor people could perform the chemistry of life. Plants could not access and use the nutrients in the soil, or transform the sun's energy into food (photosynthesis), or transport food around their bodies, or build their stems, leaves, branches, fruit or flowers. Similarly, humans could not metabolize carbohydrates and proteins, or transport food and oxygen around their bodies, or maintain healthy cells and organs, or regulate their temperature or rid their bodies of wastes.

Water can almost work miracles. I once neglected some woefully potbound Cape primrose (*Streptocarpus*) for longer than I care to admit—until they had shriveled to practically nothing anyway. Just out of curiosity, I watered them and, lo, small green nubs appeared. Once repotted, they quickly put out masses of leaves and within weeks started blooming like crazy. They were probably trying desperately to reproduce in case I threatened them with extinction again!

Our dependence on water goes back to the primordial ooze. As one of the four primary elements, water figures in every tale of creation, and every civilization seems to have a flood story. Seen as homes of the spirits, springs were called "dreaming sites" and were often venerated as sacred sources of healing. The ancient Egyptians, Greeks and Japanese believed in warm baths as therapy to heal wounds, relieve fatigue and raise the spirits, as did the Romans, who were famous for their elaborate *Thermae*, complete with hot showers, plunge pools and masseurs. People still throng to spas such as Baden-Baden (the Romans' *Aquae Areliae*) to "take the waters."

Water's powers extended to conferring immortality, at least if you believed in the Fountain of Youth; Spanish explorer Ponce de León (c.1460–1521) did, so the legend goes, and spent a good part of his life trying to find it (in Florida, of all places). Then there was the Bavarian priest, Sebastian Kniepp (1821–1897), whose *water cure* included walking barefoot in wet grass for 15 to 45 minutes a day to stimulate the nervous and circulatory systems.[1]

Whether you doff your socks or not, water—the giver of life, the symbol of grace—belongs in every healing garden. Not only is it an essential element in nature's fabric as a whole, it is also endlessly beguiling. Nothing brings more life to a garden than water. Everything gravitates to it. Plants dispatch their roots posthaste to moist areas; animals, especially birds, flock to it; and people, mesmerized by its spell, find themselves quite carried away.

Water Works

Whatever your garden's size or shape, there is a way to bring in water's quicksilver enchantment.

Reflecting pools A calm reflecting pool adds a magical dimension to a meditative space. Bringing the sky to earth and enveloping it in greenery, the pool mirrors reality yet turns it upside down and makes it oddly elastic. Gazing into its depths (or is that heights?) gives new meaning to perspective. On a more earthly note, be careful not to let the water stagnate or become a mosquito breeding ground.

A reflecting pool adds a magical perspective and calmness to any space.

Ponds, Pools and Puddles Any sort of water feature will be a magnet for birds, insects, frogs and toads, beetles and dragonflies. If you don't have room for a pond or waterfall, get a bird bath; it can be a bowl type on a pedestal or simply a water-filled depression in a rock. Then wait for the avian parade. I've watched a flock of young starlings come in, and literally line up waiting for their turn in the bath. Regular flapping of wings and much whistling informed the current occupant his time was up. Make sure to keep the birdbath clean, scrubbing out any algae regularly. I also have the "soggy crumb problem" to deal with—the local crows are masterful scavengers of discarded fast-food buns and bread, but, disliking hard crusts, bring them to my bird bath and dunk them like the best biscotti.

Water Vessels A half barrel, ceramic pot or even a small basin can bring water's freshness to your garden, or sitting space. One of the most charming water features I have seen was a generously wide but fairly shallow terracotta bowl with a clump of dwarf papyrus (*Cyperus*)and some silky smooth stones the colors of sand and earth.

Natural Water A large natural pond is an all-season attraction, for you and for wildlife. If you can, establish an area where the bank gradually slopes into the pond so that small animals can drink. If the pond is large enough, they will not prey on its inhabitants.

Moving Water Be it bubbler, waterfall, fountain or meandering stream, moving water quiets the mind and soothes the soul. Cooling and calming, it is nevertheless animated and conveys a sense of going somewhere, of seeking a way, of carrying things along. My spirits are always buoyed by the sound of water and its promise of refreshment and renewal.

The trickling-brook effect can be achieved by making water tumble over a series of stepped rocks down a slope. As long as it doesn't resemble a Giant's Causeway plunked down in the middle of a meadow, this can provide a glorious moving picture to match the sound, and lots of edge area for planting. (See "On the Edge," Chapter 5.) In limited spaces, greenhouses or conservatories, there are sculptural fountains tiered like a multi-level cakeserver, or molded fibreglass components called *flowforms* that create a similar effect. Not only will they add ambient sound but the plants will love the higher humidity and regulated temperature.

Water, especially moving water, not only looks and sounds cooling, it actually is. As warm air moves over it, the water evaporates. Water molecules suspended in the air as water vapor capture heat energy, cooling the air in the process. Waterfalls and waves on the beach are natural forms of white noise (technically, a sound that contains every frequency within the range of human hearing). Certain audio frequencies in white noise have a definite calming effect, which is why meditation CDs feature surf sounds, rain, etc. (They're also recommended for colicky babies, I hear).

The splish-splash of water also acts to mask unwelcome sounds. Combined with a screening of trees and shrubs, a fountain or cascade provides welcome white noise, and an aural distraction from traffic or the city's hum and bustle. To know water's beauty and fascination, one has only to see children head immediately for the smallest boggy-bottomed ditch, or hordes of office-workers cluster around a public fountain, a pale but welcome substitute for a natural water source in a sea of concrete and asphalt.

Water splish-splashing over rocks cools the air, buoys the spirits and masks unwanted sounds.

- Figure out how big you want your pond and then make it twice the size. Otherwise, I guarantee you'll be wishing you had made it bigger.
- Ponds can be free-form and lined with heavy plastic, or a rigid pre-formed unit sunk into the ground, or poured concrete or natural.
- Plants and fish prefer a pond at least 20 inches (50 cm) deep because it stays cooler and less clouded with algae. It should be at least 3 feet (90 cm) deep if you want to leave the fish outside over winter.
- You need a mixture of submerged oxygenating plants such as anacharis (*Elodea*) and water milfoil (*Myriophyllum* spp.) as well as floating plants such as water lettuce (*Pistia stratiotes*) and water lilies (*Nymphaea* spp.) to keep the pond healthy and the water clear. A fountain or waterfall will also help oxygenate the water.
- Set containers of yellow flag (*Iris pseudacorus*), papyrus (*Cyperus*), taro (*Colocasia* spp.), etc. on built-in ledges or on submerged, overturned pots.
- Flowering water plants such as water lilies need at least six hours of sunshine.
- Provide a stick or two (just stuck in the bottom or in one of your pots of water plants) for dragonflies to perch on.
- If you have a large natural pond, plant the banks with a diversity of suitable native plants and grasses that will hold the soil and offer rich habitat for all sorts of creatures. Provide flat rocks as perching platforms and basking places for birds and amphibians.

Groundwater

One of the most compelling reasons not to throw a lot of chemicals about is to avoid contaminating the groundwater. We know about surface water—lakes, ponds and streams—but what is groundwater? As it sounds, groundwater is the water *under* the soil surface, saturating the spaces between rock and soil usually to a depth of about 325 feet (100 m). (The term *water table* refers to the top level of groundwater saturation.) About a quarter of Canadians (including *all* of Prince Edward Island's residents) depend on groundwater for all their daily water needs while 50 per cent of U.S. citizens rely on it for their drinking water. As the deaths in Walkerton, Ontario, in 2000 graphically showed, groundwater contamination can be devastating. Not only that, but the groundwater eventually carries any pollutants into lakes and rivers, upon which the rest of the North American population relies.

Groundwater moves at varying rates depending on how permeable the soil and rock formations are. In some places it might move several feet (more than a

meter) a day; in others, just a couple of inches (5 cm) a century. Water can spend as little as a few days underground or as long as tens or even hundreds of thousands of years (once the latter is contaminated, it's essentially blighted forever). Rivers, by contrast, renew themselves completely in about two weeks. Interestingly, because the underground topography is a whole different world, groundwater doesn't always flow in the same direction as surface water; this means pollutants can be carried off to somewhere quite unexpected.

Areas with lots of loose material and therefore a useful supply of water are called *aquifers* (this is what dowsers look for when you want to dig a well). Groundwater flowing through aquifers is naturally filtered and usually free of disease-causing microorganisms, but major influxes of animal wastes, applications of agricultural chemicals, leaks from underground storage tanks or heavy road salting can easily override the natural processes. For example, just one quart (1 L) of gasoline can contaminate 260,000 gallons (1 million L) of groundwater.[2]

Groundwater is a critical part of the water cycle, constantly flowing into streams, rivers, lakes and wetlands (one of the most biodiverse and fragile ecosystems), and

Rocks surrounding a pond offer perching platforms and basking places for birds and amphibians.

being replenished by rain and snow. When we cover the land with asphalt and buildings, we interrupt that life-giving cycle, and simply divert the rain (now laden with pollution from those streets and buildings) directly into the surface water. By protecting the skin of the earth with mulch and a living blanket of plants, we allow much more rain and snow to soak into the ground, not only benefiting the plants but also replenishing one of our most precious, if hidden, resources.

We North Americans are incredibly lucky to have the lion's share of the world's fresh water. But not only are we cavalier about polluting it, we are positively wasteful in our use of it. According to the American Water Works Association, the average American uses 74 gallons (280 L) a day, just indoors, while Canadians are even bigger waterhogs at 86 gallons (326 L) a day. Come summer, a staggering 50 to 75 per cent of municipally treated water is poured on to lawns and gardens.[3] As the climate changes, more areas are subject to extremes of heat, drought (and yes, flooding), and watering restrictions are common.

Wise use of water is vital and, with careful planning, your garden can thrive on a lot less. This is not to say that you shouldn't grow moisture-loving plants. See

Be Water Wise

- Mulch, mulch, mulch. It helps the soil absorb and hold water, and prevents evaporation and erosion. (See Chapter 2 for more on mulch.)
- Use drip irrigation or soaker hoses rather than overhead sprinklers which lose 30 per cent or more water to evaporation.
- Water by hand. It's time-consuming but allows you to get the water right to the root system.
- Water in the early morning or late afternoon, but allow time to let the foliage dry off before nightfall.
- Occasional deep watering is much better for all plants than frequent shallow watering. But don't overwater; unless they are adapted to it, plants can drown if their roots are sitting in water.
- Containers and pots dry out very quickly and may need watering once or twice a day. Line the containers with cocofibre or newspapers to hold water in and use a potting mix with water-retaining polymers.
- Get a rain barrel and capture as much rainwater as you can. Disconnect downspouts from their underground links and redirect the water onto your garden, or into a barrel. A 1,000-square-foot (93 m²) rooftop can collect more than 400 gallons (1,514 L) from one inch (2.54 cm) of rain.[4]

if your garden has a low area that naturally stays moist and group them there. Carve out a space close to the water source where you can concentrate water just where it's needed. Or create a bog garden next to your pond. And, as I urge in Chapter 5, forgo large, water-guzzling expanses of lawn.

Let It Rain

Have you ever noticed that, no matter how much you water your plants with the hose, nothing gives them a boost like rainwater? After a rain, everything looks preternaturally green and fresh. It should because rain carries with it a good shot of nitrogen, the key nutrient for green growth. There's lots of nitrogen in the air all the time, but plants can't access it. It takes lightning's extreme heat to zap the atmospheric nitrogen with hydrogen or oxygen creating ammonium and nitrate (two forms of nitrogen). These are dissolved in moisture and carried to the ground in rain, in a form plants can use. Besides nitrogen, rain brings sulfur (as much as 40 pounds/18 kg an acre a year), needed for plant amino acids. And it washes down dust—dust which has often traveled from distant continents and which can contain a smorgasbord of plant treats: potash from the ash produced by forest fires, for instance, and minerals from volcanic dust. Rain also doesn't have the chlorine that treated water does; it is warmer (plants don't like a freezing shower any more than we do) and has a lower pH (usually 5.6, or slightly acid). (See Chapter 2 for more on pH.)

Acid rain, which eats away at plants and buildings, and poisons the ecosystems of lakes and rivers, has a pH of less than five. It's created when the air pollutants, sulfur dioxide and nitrogen oxide (produced primarily by the burning of fossil fuels in our cars, industries, gas mowers and blowers, etc.), react with water, oxygen and oxidants in the atmosphere to form solutions of sulfuric acid and nitric acid. Acid rain is a serious problem—one scientist says Germany's Black Forest truly is black, since so many evergreens have been killed by acid rain, leaving just the black trunks—so every scrap of fossil-fuel reduction helps.[5]

Xeriscaping

All plants need water, but not all plants need the same amount of water. The idea of "dry gardening" is called *xeriscaping* from the Greek word *xeros* meaning dry (same as *Xerox*, which means "dry copying"). The key is to use drought-tolerant plants, many of which have silver/gray, succulent or narrow leaves. Look for plants whose native habitat is dry—Mediterranean denizens such as donkey tail spurge (*Euphorbia myrsinites*) and sea holly (*Eryngium alinum*, *E. bourgatii*, and *E. giganteum*), or herbs such as lavender (*Lavandula*), or plants of semi-arid regions such as wormwood (*Artemisia*), and many of our native plants such as tickseed (*Coreopsis grandiflora*). Desert plants obviously survive drought but not our cold and wet winters. Many alpines will survive cold and drought, but suffer too from winter wet unless you have impeccable drainage. Ornamental grasses will usually tolerate dry conditions as will many junipers, sedums, poppies and salvias.

Whether a little or a lot, the simple act of watering a plant is giving life. Consider every precious drop each time you turn on the tap and have one of the billion or so glasses of water North Americans drink every day. It is a source—and force—we can't do without.

Drought-tolerant plants such as santolina thrive in a gravel-mulched xeriscape that needs little or no supplementary water.

Some Good Drought-Tolerant Plants

Thrift	*Armeria maritima*
Butterfly weed	*Asclepias tuberosa*
Blue false indigo	*Baptisia australis*
Reed grass	*Calamagrostis* x *acutiflora* 'Karl Foerster'
Threadleaf coreopsis	*Coreopsis verticillata*
Purple coneflower	*Echinacea purpurea*
Gaura	*Gaura lindheimeri*
Oxeye sunflower	*Heliopsis helianthoides*
Flax	*Linum perenne*
Sundrops	*Oenothera perennis*
Prickly pear cactus	*Opuntia lumifusus*
Moss phlox (groundcover)	*Phlox subulata*
Portulaca	*Portulaca grandiflora*
Lavender cotton	*Santolina*
Hens and chicks	*Sempervivum* spp.
Feather grass	*Stipa tenuissima*
Tamarix	*Tamarix ramosissima*

IN PRAISE OF TREES

The wonder is that we can see
these trees and not wonder more.

RALPH WALDO EMERSON

A friend describing the evolution of a gardener said that, once the infatuation with annuals is over, the passion for perennials spent, the fixation on foliage done, that is the time the mature gardener starts to grow trees from seed—such an act of faith. But trees are our links to the future and the past. To walk through an old-growth forest is to hear the echoes of centuries. To gaze at a stand of white pine is to see the proud masts of the tall ships. To stand under the spreading canopy of an oak or beech is to know it will provide shelter for generations to come.

From totems and travises to Home Depot's stack of two-by-fours, from voyageurs' canoes to sounding boards, from cedar tea, which saved so many from scurvy, to *taxol*, the yew (*Taxus*) derivative which is a potential weapon against cancer, the forest has been an abundant source of building materials, food, fertilizers, fuels, medicine and magic. Topping the list of most used North American native plants compiled by ethnobotanist Daniel Moerman is Western red cedar (*Thuja plicata*) with 368 different uses, including 52 as drugs and 188 as fibre alone.[1] Cedar may have been named *arbor vitae*, but in fact *all* trees are trees of life.

So much of the garden's restorative power comes from trees, from their greenery, their deep seasonal rhythms, their solidity and strength, their mystery and their beauty. Witness the ancient Egyptian who, around 1400 BC, had this inscribed on his tomb: "That each day I may walk unceasingly on the banks of my water, that my soul may repose on the branches of the trees which I planted, that I may refresh myself under the shadow of my sycamore." Or consider the group of modern school children who, when asked what they would most like to have in their playground expanse of pavement and beaten grass, replied, "Shade and a place to sit."

We tend to be amazingly cavalier about our trees, on local and global scales. Too often, they are regarded as permanent fixtures that will withstand any amount of abuse and neglect, or dispensed with to add that oh-so-necessary bedroom extension. Someone once said that the suburbs are where developers bulldoze all the trees and then name streets after them. Tree expert Dr. Alex Shigo describes a tree on a U.S. golf course that was killed in an arboreal version of death of a thousand cuts. In this case, the tree died of thousands of small holes as golfers repeatedly stabbed the tree with their tees. The constant assault eventually destroyed the cambium, the living layer of cells under the bark which carry food and water between roots and canopy. It doesn't take much to destroy the complex balance of a tree's ecosystem, yet people seem to keep finding ever new and different ways to do it.

Part of our cavalier attitude can be found in the language we use about trees. We seem to regard them, like soil, as inanimate things, rather than complex living structures harboring sophisticated chemical and transportation systems, providing shelter for a range of inhabitants, and having an enormous impact on air and water quality. Indeed, our lives depend on them. Yet, we call dead trees "firewood," instead of what University of Guelph interpretive horticulturist Henry Kock refers to as "bed and breakfast" for wildlife. Something surplus and useless is termed "dead wood"; we call forest duff "leaf litter," as though it were nature's empty cigarette packages or pop bottles to be cleaned up; we describe lack of action as sitting "like a bump on a log," and deride someone as being "thick as a plank."

Trees: Wonders of the World

Yet trees not only create a habitable, aesthetically pleasing environment, they also provide shade, give us fruit, nuts, flowers and glorious fall color, moderate urban climates, improve air quality, increase property values, nurture wildlife, produce oxygen and sequester carbon, and reduce stormwater runoff.

But trees' most powerful impact is on the climate. If soil is the skin of the earth, then trees are the lungs. Every leaf on these fantastically complex plants is a little oxygen factory, keeping the air we breathe breathable. (A 115-year-old beech exposes about 200,000 leaves with a total surface of about 1,435 square yards/1,200 square meters.[2]) This happens through the most vital manufacturing process on earth—photosynthesis, a process scientists have never been able to replicate. In the leaf cells tiny structures called *chloroplasts* contain the "lifeblood" of plants: green chlorophyll (the stuff that is chemically so similar to our blood). It captures the radiant energy from sunlight and, with water drawn up from the roots and carbon dioxide from the air, converts

In spring, Florida dogwood (Cornus florida) *lights up the woodlands with its lustrous pink blooms.*

it to chemical energy for food. The deceptively simple equation is: *Carbon dioxide (CO_2) plus water (H_2O) (with chlorophyll and sunlight) equals glucose and oxygen.* The glucose produced is combined with other chemicals to make other sugars and carbohydrates as well as proteins, fats and oils; the oxygen is released, enriching the air for the likes of us.

In the next step (respiration), the trees use oxygen to break down the glucose to access the energy as food. In so doing, they release carbon dioxide and water (the reverse of photosynthesis). This constant recycling is critical to their health and the planet's health. In a perfect world, levels of all these elements would be in balance. But that rarely happens, in no small measure due to human activity, as well as natural events.

Measuring the amounts of carbon dioxide and oxygen is difficult since it depends on the age, size and health of the tree and all the environmental variables, but David Nowak of the U.S. Forests Service estimates that a single 20-inch- (50 cm) diameter tree in Brooklyn takes in 157 pounds (71 kg) of carbon dioxide, sequesters 43 pounds (19.5 kg) of carbon and produces 115 pounds (52 kg) of oxygen a year.[3]

Trees do an enormous amount of air conditioning; a single 20-inch diameter tree can take in 157 pounds of carbon dioxide and produce 115 pounds of oxygen a year.

Since the average person uses about 400 pounds (181.4 kg) of oxygen a year, it would take just four such trees to supply all their oxygen needs. Of course, if four trees disappear, it doesn't mean that one person drops dead; in fact, the waters of the world (and the algae in them) are the principal oxygen generators, but trees' contribution is significant, particularly in urban centers.

Trees rival Filter Queens when it comes to air pollution: the sickly soup of carbon monoxide, sulfur dioxide, ozone and nitrogen oxides produced by our car exhaust, residential furnaces, power plants and such. In addition, trees filter out particulates such as pollen, dust, ash and smoke. A Chicago study found that 120 acres (48.5 hectares) of tree canopy absorbed up to 5.5 pounds (2.5 kg) of carbon monoxide, 127 pounds (57.6 kg) of sulfur dioxide, 24 pounds (10.8 kg) of nitrogen dioxide and 170 pounds (77 kg) of particulates a day.[4] That's in *one day*!

As we saw in Chapter 3, when sulfur dioxide and nitrogen oxides combine with water, they create sulfuric and nitric acids (acid rain). When we inhale these gases or they come in contact with our bodies, they react with the water in our lungs or eyes, and produce these acids that, at low levels, cause irritation and, at higher levels, severe damage. Trees can absorb a surprising amount of pollutants, but, like us, they will seriously suffer from overexposure (ozone restricts carbohydrate movement, for example). Visible symptoms are leaf burn, lesions, bleaching and, in the case of conifers, browning of the needles. Chronic damage undermines the tree's resistance, making it much more vulnerable to pests and disease. So, if you have a street tree nearby, be sure to give it some TLC. Urban trees are growing in unnatural conditions and are under a lot of stress.

How to Keep Your Trees Healthy

Don't take them for granted; check them on a regular basis. Look at the leaves or needles: are they the usual size, the right color? Are there signs of insects or disease? Are there broken branches or bark injuries? If the tree is stressed, determine where the problem is and deal with it promptly.

Keep grass and paving well away from the trunk; mulch and leave the leaves or chop them and mix them with well-rotted manure or wood chips. It's hard to add too much organic matter—remember there are a lot of mouths to feed in that root zone!

Give newly planted trees a two- to four-inch (five- to 10-cm) deep layer of mulch in a three- or four-foot (90- to 120-cm) circle (bigger if possible) around, but not touching, the trunk. (See Chapter 2 for more on mulch.)

Water if necessary in periods of drought. Newly planted trees should be watered regularly until they are established.

Avoid compacting the soil around trees; if they are surrounded by paving, take extra pains to water and fertilize. Asphalt is not a mulch.

Prune the trees properly from the outset. Get a good reference book or professional advice. Keep in mind that for the kindest cuts, you should:

- train most trees to have a single leader.
- remove dead, diseased and crossing branches.
- never cut too close to the trunk; cut at the branch collar, the slightly bulbous area at the base of each branch. This area contains a natural protective chemical zone that will callus over the wound and heal it naturally. Do not slather the wound with any kind of gunk or sealer.
- never lop the top off a tree. If it's going to hit the power lines or overwhelm your house, move it while it's still relatively small.
- never allow someone to climb your trees using spikes.

Without trees, the water cycle would be going nowhere. By taking water in their roots and transpiring it into the atmosphere, they create the more humid, cooler environment we gravitate to in summer, ice cream in hand. In the northern states and Canada, you can reduce air-conditioning and heating costs dramatically by planting large deciduous trees on the south side of your house which will keep the house cool in summer, yet allow the warmth of the winter sun to reach the building.

Urban trees help to offset the "heat island" effect created by the vast expanses of paving, asphalt, and concrete and glass buildings which absorb solar radiation. Cities are 5 to 9 degrees F (3 to 5 degrees C) warmer than the surrounding undeveloped areas (no one who's ever been stuck in rush hour traffic will be surprised to learn that paved surfaces in summer can reach a sweltering 120 degrees F/ 49 degrees C[5]). Rain, which once went into the soil, runs off into gutters and pipes, or dries up on the surface. So it is left to trees to draw up hundreds of gallons of water from underground and, in transpiring it, temper the fever. They also work at night when the air temperature drops and the radiation starts moving from the ground upwards. Then, their generous canopies enfold the earth and slow down the radiation.

Not all that rain is lost, however. A University of California study measured how much rainfall was intercepted by a nine-year-old callery pear tree, 28 feet (8.5 m) tall with a 19-foot (5.8 m) crown covering 276 square feet (25.6 m²) The storm dumped half an inch (1.3 cm) of rain, or 86.1 gallons (326 L) in the measured area, of which the tree intercepted an impressive 58.1 gallons (220 L) or 68 per cent.[6]

Trees' extensive root systems also help prevent erosion (and don't believe those who say a tree's roots only extend as far as the dripline; in fact, the root system can be three times wider than the canopy). Strong anchor roots go deep into the ground, but most of the feeder roots are in the top foot of soil. This is why it is so important to mulch and leave the leaves to add precious organic matter to the soil, hold in moisture and moderate the temperature. On a trip to London's Kew Gardens, I noticed that picnickers had to choose between grass and shade because the entire area under every tree's canopy had been thickly mulched (and sported polite little signs explaining why).

Trees' climate-controlling abilities also include the wind, which unchecked can be not only downright uncomfortable for the gardener but also damaging to

other plants. Trees (or a hedge) slow the gusts down and break them up into gentler breezes. In urban settings, trees can buffer us from the cacophony of honks, sirens and screeches. The greatest reductions of traffic noise, along a main highway for example, require belts of trees from 35 to 100 feet (10 to 30 meters) wide. But by berming the soil up and planting trees, shrubs and understory plants along it, noise can be cut by nearly half. Near our house, a busy highway was lined with large cement-block noise barriers. Rows of small trees were planted along them in an effort to hide their ugly expanses and perhaps mitigate the pollution. However, imprisoned in an exhaust-filled corridor, smothered in salt-laden snow in winter and baked against the concrete walls in summer, many have perished. Trees can do a lot, but not the impossible.

In our own gardens, where space is usually more limited, a few big trees interplanted with large shrubs can be an effective noise barrier and screen. If that isn't feasible, a hedge (either deciduous or evergreen) can work, too. A wall of greenery will provide the sense of enclosure and privacy so vital to a healing space.

Deciduous trees, evergreens and flowering shrubs not only create a stunning tapestry of form and color but also act as a buffer against noise and pollution.

And what's good for the individual is also good on a larger scale. Neighborhoods with lots of greenery and trees are not only perceived as being better, they suffer less vandalism, littering and crime. The people living there are happier and healthier, even if they don't acknowledge their debt to their green protectors. And homes with trees and verdant landscaping go up in value. (See Chapter 11 for more on urban greening.)

Into the Woods

One of the historic Rothschilds once said, "Every garden no matter how small should have at least one acre of woodland."

"Ha," say those of us gardening in our little postage-stamp Edens. But even with just one or two big trees, it's possible to get a woodland feel. Big trees are too often just marooned in an expanse of lawn (remember how we love to recreate

One of the Rothschilds once said, "Every garden no matter how small should have at least one acre of woodland." There are few landscapes so magical, and even with just one or two trees, you can cast a woodland spell.

the savanna archetype). Far better to bring diversity, life and a symphony of textures with a dense planting and perhaps a little clearing. What could be more magical than your own glade?

More demand for shade plants means a much better supply is now available, including many native plants. Visualize how nature puts together plants in the forest and duplicate those layers, from the canopy of the tallest trees, to the understory trees such as dogwoods (*Cornus*) and redbuds (*Cercis canadensis*), then the woodland shrubs such as rhododendrons (*Rhododendron*) if the soil is acid enough, or jetbead (*Rhodotypos scandens*), viburnum (*Viburnum*), winterberry (*Ilex verticillata*), buttonbush (*Cephalanthus occidentalis*), laurels (*Kalmia*), etc., and finally the delicate ferns, Solomon's seal (*Polygonatum*), baneberries (*Actaea*), epimediums (*Epimedium*), merrybells (*Uvularia*), foamflowers (*Tiarella*) and mosses.

In my garden, we took up all the grass around a large sugar maple and a small birch stand, we used the sod in berms around the edge and then top-dressed with a thick layer of manure and triple mix, along with all the maple leaves (well shredded). We let that sit for a winter and by spring the soil was workable. We planted the layers as described above and then mulched with a layer of fine wood chips. I've added a couple of logs to rot down, and each year I shred the leaves and tuck in more spring ephemeral bulbs.

One day, gardening near the house, I watched two young lads, deep in conversation, cut across the corner to walk along the path through my little woodland, their heads close together, intent on "important boy business." I was immensely gratified to see they found the path so inviting and used it so naturally. Another time, I hope they pause to check out the strange raspberry-like fruits of the dogwood or the black beetles scurrying equally intently through the leaves.

Essential Evergreens

With the heavy emphasis on winter in the northern states and Canada, evergreens (conifers and broad-leaved) are a must. They offer fabulous form (pyramid, globe, column, mound, drooping), as well as texture (ferny, rough, lacy, prickly) and color (gray, blue, yellow and every shade of green). The *witch's broom* hunters have been busy tracking down dwarf varieties to fit even the smallest garden. (Conifers occasionally send out an odd shoot with densely clustered needles quite different from the rest of the tree; these *witch's brooms*, as they're called, are removed—often by a

Although many people regard "winter interest" as an oxymoron, they would have to admit that few scenes are as beautiful as a stand of snow-dusted evergreens.

well-aimed shotgun blast since they can occur many feet above the ground—then rooted and cloned.) There's an evergreen for almost every type of soil and exposure. They extend shelter and protection for wildlife and really do provide winter interest (a phrase I know many people regard as an oxymoron).

Although evergreens give a garden stability and permanence, they still mark the seasons. In spring, there is no fresher green than the yew's (*Taxus*) new clothes, while the slender 'Gold Cone' juniper (*Juniperus communis* 'Gold Cone') looks as though the fairies have decorated it with tiny yellow lights. In summer, a 'Fat Albert' blue spruce (*Picea pungens* 'Fat Albert') struts its color against the dark purple of 'Forest Pansy' redbud (*Cercis canadensis* 'Forest Pansy'). In fall, the Siberian cypress (*Microbiota decussata*) turns a rusty burgundy, and in winter, nothing holds the snow more picturesquely than a stand of regal spruce (*Picea*).

The best time to plant a tree was 25 years ago, the second best time is today. If you move into an area with no trees, first amend the soil and then get planting. But do your homework; check out a tree's charms and vices, and choose wisely. Unless you have lots of room, resist those "cute little blue spruces"—that's a real oxymoron. By putting one of those behemoths in a small front yard, you are merely dooming it to be deprived of its spreading skirts, limbed up like a lollipop, then chopped down. Look for a relatively dwarf cultivar, such as 'Tiffin' (*P. p.* 'Tiffin') and the aforementioned 'Fat Albert.'

Allelopathy or The Black Walnut Problem

Many gardeners have struggled to garden under black walnut trees, only to see their plantings fade and die, poisoned by a toxin called *juglone* which is secreted by the tree's roots. Similarly, the opportunistic tree of heaven (*Ailanthus*), an invasive exotic from China, uses chemicals in its leaves, stem and roots to beat out competition, successfully invading forests as well as every urban alleyway.

This chemical warfare is called *allelopathy*, the process in which plants, as well as microorganisms, produce substances to gain advantage in the battle to survive. These allelochemicals may kill other plant roots, inhibit photosynthesis or reduce cholorophyll, all pretty well guaranteed to do the neighbors in. Since nature is ever creative, the allelochemicals may be released as a gas through the stomata on the leaves; or as the leaves or needles decompose; or as a root excretion. They are part of the simmering chemical stew that both feeds and destroys the millions of microorganisms in the soil, particularly in the rhizosphere.

Aggressive, yes, but there is a defensive aspect, too. Many plants concentrate allelochemicals in their fruit, seeds and pollen, which protects these vital reproductive elements from damage. Allelochemicals in roots, leaves and the all-important phloem tissue are produced at higher levels when the plant is under stress, in an effort to ensure survival. Plants' chemical changes also allow them to communicate: acacia trees and lima beans, to name two, release volatile compounds when they are being munched on. Other trees pick up the message and start marshalling their chemical defenses against the predators. (Amazingly, if the plant is simply damaged by, for instance, the wind, the compounds are still released but totally ignored by the neighbors.)

Allelopathy is one reason to rotate crops in your veggie garden. For instance, cruciferous vegetables such as cabbage and broccoli have a chemical called *thiocyanate*

Some Plants That Will Grow Under Black Walnut Trees

Astilbe (*Astilbe*)	Pulmonaria (*Pulmonaria*)
Bee balm (*Monarda*)	Sedum (*Sedum*)
Bellflower (*Campanula*)	Lambs' ears (*Stachys*)
Crested wood fern (*Dryopteris cristata*)	Trillium (*Trillium*)
Daylilies (*Hemerocallis*)	Violets (*Viola*)
Leopard's bane (*Doronicum*)	Japanese maple (*Acer palmatum*)
Sweet woodruff (*Galium odoratum*)	February daphne (*Daphne mezereum*)
Coralbells (*Heuchera*)	Rose of Sharon (*Hibiscus syriacus*)
Siberian iris (*Iris sibirica*)	Canadian hemlock (*Tsuga canadensis*)

in their leaves, a natural defense against bugs; however, when those leaves decay and enter the soil, the thiocyanate released can affect subsequent plantings. (For more on vegetables, see Chapter 8.) Some plants can even poison themselves. If your asparagus starts committing vegetal hara-kiri, it may be because of an excess of allelochemicals in its bed. If planted too closely together, cucumbers will try to kill each other, and fruit farmers know that they can't replant apple and peach trees where others have died because of the toxins left in the soil.

The plus side to allelopathy is that some plants such as oats, sunflowers, cucumbers, sweet potatoes and the cover crops of barley, rye and wheat produce allelochemicals that discourage weeds. So, encircling your vegetable garden with sunflowers is weed-suppressing as well as decorative. Mind you, weeds such as crabgrass and ragweed fight back with allelochemicals of their own that can inhibit vegetable seeds. Research is being done on harnessing these allelochemicals as natural herbicides—which would be a major step toward getting our gardens off synthetic chemicals.

Don't despair if you have a black walnut tree; it's not toxic to all plants by any means, and many shrubs and perennials will live quite happily in its dappled shade. A tree that can only be described as tall, dark and handsome, the black walnut can easily top 100 feet (30.5 m), boasts deep gray/brown furrowed bark and has a surprisingly delicate leaf texture. So desirable is its wood for fine cabinetry that, in fact, you should consider it a prized possession.

Trees have a profound effect on our gardens, our communities and the world. One of the most significant actions you can take in your garden is planting a tree—a real tree such as beech, oak, fir or redwood. As Proust wrote, we can learn a great deal from "that vigorous and pacific tribe in whose gracious company we spend so many cool, silent and intimate hours."

5

VARIETY IS LIFE

*You can't make a centipede
by gluing ants together.*

GREG TITUS, 1985

Variety is said to be the spice of life, but it would be more accurate to say variety *is* life. Biodiversity (meaning what it says, "a diversity of life") is what keeps the heart of this world beating, what drives its rhythms and sustains its energy. As we have seen, every living thing is a vital brick in the overall edifice. Every ecosystem, from a teaspoon of humus to a rain forest, is an intricate web of links and connections, and every ecosystem is part of the world ecosystem or ecosphere. The more diversity at every level, i.e., the more processes and interactions going on, the richer the ecosystem becomes in nutrients, energy, fertility—life. And with increasing complexity, the ecosystem gets ever closer to a state of stability and harmony.

Biodiversity is a triple-decker affair: we need diversity in genetic material within species (see "Heritage Seeds" in Chapter 8); we need diversity of species (plant and animal) and we need diversity of ecosystems, the three-dimensional places harboring life. On top of that, we need the diverse functions that organisms carry out, and of course the so-called abiotic (non-living) but equally crucial components: rock, soil, sediment, water and air.

So far, we have identified about 1.5 million life forms on earth, out of what may be as many as 80 million (though most estimates peg the number at around 10 million). The tropics are the richest in biodiversity but Canada has recorded more than 100,000 species (not counting viruses)[1] and the U.S. counts more than double that. There may be as many again still awaiting discovery. Some of them will never be recorded because they will be extinct before our scientific efforts get to them.

As ecosystems are altered through climate changes, natural disasters and human manipulation, diversity is lost and the ecosystem, in turn, is weakened. In the past 250 years, Canada has lost such creatures as the great auk and the blue pike, and currently more than 100 species of plants and animals are endangered—that we know of. In the United States, 200 species have been lost and some 5,000 are at risk.[2] In areas such as the North with simpler ecosystems, the loss of one species has greater impact than a similar loss in a rain-forest ecosystem. The loss of an entire ecosystem is devastating. In Canada, through agriculture and urbanization, we have but scant remains of tallgrass prairie and Carolinian forest, for instance; 68 per cent of Ontario's species-rich wetlands are gone as are 65 per cent of Atlantic coastal marshes, while the destruction of the West Coast's old-growth forest has been

Diversity Defined

Biodiversity
The variety of life and its interconnected processes in an area.

Ecosystem
A community of interacting plants and animals in an area considered together with their environment, including minerals, soil, water and sunlight, all linked by two major forces: the flow of energy and the cycling of nutrients.

well documented.[3] In the United States, nearly 60 per cent of the country (excluding Alaska) has lost most of its natural vegetation.[4]

Of course, ecosystems are always evolving and there is such a thing as natural extinction. In striving for balance, nature is constantly changing and adapting. The difference is time. Before humans, ecological change was measured in thousands of years. Plants and animals had a chance to adapt, to modify themselves, to move to more favorable conditions. Human activity has been concentrated into scant centuries, if that, and we have spread like invasive weeds over the globe.

We may shrug over the loss of a bug here or a wildflower there, because we don't immediately see any effect. But our knowledge is so woefully incomplete, we can't know what the ultimate effect may be. Aldo Leopold, the father of environmental thinking, wrote that keeping every cog and wheel is the first precaution of intelligent tinkering. Keep all the parts because they could be a lot more vital than you think. Glue together all the ants you like; they'll never make a centipede.

But in urging conservation, there is the case of "species considered inimical to human interests: How many species of mosquito do we want to preserve—do hay fever sufferers care about preserving the full genetic potential of ragweed?"[5] The problem is that these questions are posed strictly in "me, me, me" terms. The importance of preserving biodiversity goes far beyond selfish human concerns. Too often, the justification is based on dollar values in the market place, making it all too easy to dismiss this tree or that plant on the grounds that it is "useless." Nothing in nature is useless, just as nothing in nature is wasted. We simply may not know what the use is. And every living thing, even ragweed, plays a valuable— and priceless—role in the ecosphere.

There is a certain amount of redundancy built into ecosystems—more than one species performing a similar function, for example. This enables the ecosystem to survive a loss here and there, with no apparent ill effect. But in the

Every member in this woodland plant community has a role to play in preserving the richness and health of the ecosystem.

A garden is full of microclimates—
beside a gravel path, next to a
large rock, on a slight slope—that
create diverse growing conditions
for a host of different plants.

long term, resistance and resilience are weakened. And once an ecosystem is lost, there is no guarantee that, even if all interference is halted and it is left to its own devices, it will ever return.

This is not to say that we haven't been gaining species, species that have been either deliberately or accidentally brought in, but often, as with kudzu, wild oats and zebra mussels, they're more bane than boon (see Chapter 6 for more). The point is that "the conservation of biodiversity is not a numbers game; a species gained does not make up for one that is lost."[6] And real diversity is not just the number of species, but also their relative abundance; for instance, a stand of 10 oaks, 10 maples, and 10 poplars is richer than 28 oaks, one maple and one poplar.

Microclimates: Pockets of Diversity

So how can such a vast variety of organisms exist within even tiny areas in an ecosystem? One of the reasons is microclimates, literally "very small climates." Sometimes we will plant two or three of the same shrub or perennial in our gardens, maybe only a few feet apart. Two will thrive and the third will be a runt. We

Making Microclimates Work for You

- Know how the sun moves about your garden over the course of the day. Site your seating areas accordingly, whether you want to relax in the sun with your morning coffee or find a shady spot for afternoon meditation.
- Avoid planting tender annuals or perennials in low areas that could become frost pockets.
- South- and west-facing slopes tend to be warmer with good drainage. Small bulbs, herbs and many rock plants will relish such conditions.
- Take advantage of buildings. Plant espaliered fruit trees, for instance, on a warm south wall. On the east side, use plants such as magnolia (*Magnolia*) and Japanese maple (*Acer palmatum*) that like morning sun but need protection from the hot afternoon sun. Plant trees and evergreens on the north side as a buffer against the coldest winds, and on the west side, choose plants that will take the hotter sun and westerly breezes.
- On windy sites, plant trees, shrubs and evergreens as a windbreak, or, if space is limited, build a fence. A fence with open latticework or spaces between the boards is best. A solid fence merely creates strong turbulence which can be damaging to plants.
- Evergreens provide shade, privacy, and shelter for you and other growing things. Someone once wrote that a third of the woody plants in a garden should be evergreen, and I think that's a pretty good rule.
- Remember that paved surfaces can be real hot spots; plants grown nearby or in pots should be heat-tolerant—lavender (*Lavandula*), portulaca (*Portulaca*) and spurge (*Euphorbia*), for example. If there are wet areas, look for plants that don't mind wet feet, such as butterbur (*Petasites*), astilbe (*Astilbe*), rodgersia (*Rodgersia*), yellow flag (*Iris pseudacorus*) and ligularia (*Ligularia*).
- Plant small bulbs such as scilla (*Scilla*), glory of the snow (*Chionodoxa*) and small iris (*Iris reticulata*) under deciduous trees where they will form pools of color, blooming in the sun before the trees leaf out.

Yellow flag (Iris pseudacorus) *and butterbur* (Petasites) *don't mind wet feet, so are naturals for a soggy spot.*

have planted them the same way, played no favorites in our treatment, so why? Even within that small space, the conditions can vary: perhaps the runt is in a wetter/drier spot, exposed to just that much more/less sun, closer to a greedy competitive root system or vulnerable to a tad more wind.

Look around your garden and see how temperature, humidity, wind and frost can vary from spot to spot. Under a deciduous tree, for example, the soil is drier and it is obviously shadier. As we saw in Chapter 4, trees keep the air more humid and cooler during the day, then trap the earth's heat at night, creating microclimates for smaller plants.

Dark, humus-rich soil retains more warmth and water than light-colored, quick-draining sandy soil. Gravel and stones hold heat yet keep the earth cool and moist beneath. Impatiens (*Impatiens*), which normally shrinks from full sun, will grow extravagantly in the open if it's next to a large rock that affords a cool root run. Pools and ponds have their own ripple effect. The water not only evaporates, increasing the humidity in the area, but also holds heat, releasing it at night.

Topography begets all sorts of microclimates, even small slopes and valleys, where the plants growing on one side of the hill differ markedly from the plants on the other side. High spots in your garden are likely windier and drier. Low spots collect water and, on sunny days, can become heat pockets, several degrees warmer than the ambient air. In cold weather, however, because cold air sinks, they become frost pockets. Even the air temperature at ground level on the lee side of a rock can be several degrees higher than the moving air just above.

One of the smallest microclimates lies inside the bright bowl of a crocus (*Crocus*). The shiny petals open wide to draw in every bit of warmth from the spring sun; the cup shape acts like a satellite dish, focusing the heat in the center, and holding it when the petals close come nightfall. The temperature inside the crocus can be as much as 12 degrees F (7 degrees C) warmer than the air outside, and it often becomes a snug refuge for early-emerging insects.

On the Edge

Among the liveliest microclimates are those on the "edges," that is, the areas where borders meet. For example, the transitional area between meadow and wood; the shoreline between land and water; the slope between mountain and valley; right down to edges of lawn and flower border. Isn't the grass always the most vigorous at the edges, just where you are trying to keep it back from the plantings? And have you noticed how the plants fringing the paths, or on the perimeter of the veggie bed always seem the healthiest?

Edges often contain the best of both worlds in a world of their own, with a vibrant mix of conditions, habitats and species. We can get this "edgy" energy working in our gardens by creating more fringes: make paths, ponds and planting areas full of curves, group shrubs to create thickets and carve out more growing space along walls and beside driveways. Edges are vertical, too—you can build up a berm, sculpt a sunken garden, or terrace a steep slope. When enclosing your garden with a fence or hedge, add layers of vines and grasses and perennials. Tuck in a small water feature, and provide perching and nesting for birds. If you have trees, fill in with understory shrubs and perennials, and extend the plantings out in "peninsulas" for more edge area. If you have lawn, let an irregular band of grass grow long between it and the shrubs and trees. It will soon be colonized and humming with life.

Wavy and zigzag edges are better than straight—in fact, zigzag fences will withstand stronger winds than straight ones. Nature knows this, of course. If a forest is clearcut in a straight line, it creates an unstable edge; fairly quickly, some trees will blow down, creating space for shrubs and small trees, resulting in a greater diversity and stability.[7] (Dynamic as edges are, it's a sad fact that North American forests have been so fragmented there's too much edge and not enough middle—the deep-forest ecosystem is under grave threat in many areas.)

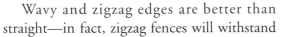

A border of mixed shrubs, trees and understory plantings form a transition zone between the garden and the outside world; this kind of "edge" planting is one of the liveliest microclimates there is.

Lawn Enough

The opposite of biodiversity is monoculture—growing just one plant. Apart from agricultural crops, the prime example of this is the great North American lawn, the expanses of grass that so many guys (it does seem to be a guy thing) feed, weed, water and worry over. As John Ingram writes, "Turf-dominated landscapes studded with the occasional exotic horticultural specimen have become the universal expression of the urban landscape.... From Halifax, N.S., to Halifax, Australia, one can find the same structural patterns and aesthetic principles, a 'blandscape' some critics have called it, endlessly repeated without regard to the regional climate, local soils, topography and other environmental constraints."[8]

The diverse mix of trees and shrubs on the left side of this pathway contrasts markedly with the flat monoculture of lawn on the right.

In North America, residential lawns cover more than 20.5 million acres (8.4 million hectares) and are doused with up to 15 times the amount of pesticides and herbicides applied to agricultural crops.[9] From 30 to 60 per cent of municipal water is used to maintain lawns—a 25-by 40-foot (7.6-by-12-m) lawn can slurp up 12,000 gallons (45,400 L) of water in a summer. And battalions of noisy, pollution-spewing power mowers, trimmers and blowers are marched out regularly to keep those millions of little grass plants in check.[10]

The prevalence of this type of landscape—trees set in grassy swards—harks back to the eighteenth-century English creation of sweeping pastoral countryside (which was in truth no more natural than LeNotre's elaborate boxwood parterres at Versailles), and more recently to the parks designed by the likes of Frederick Law Olmsted, and the waves of suburban developments that decreed every house and building be surrounded by foundation plantings, neat lawns and a tree here and there. But it goes back even further to the powerful archetype of the most favored human landscape (see Chapter 1)—the "proto-paysage" of the savanna, or open tree-studded grassland to which we have naturally gravitated since our early hunting-gathering days. Understandable as the spread of this "blandscape" may be, the fact remains that there is no such thing as a one-size-fits-all ecosystem.

As Ingram points out, this type of landscape is the closest many city-dwellers get to so-called nature. Given this distorted image, it's not surprising that people have felt detached from the larger environment, believing that nature is "wild" out there, but here it is necessarily controlled and manipulated. It's ironic that, in our subconscious insistence on recreating the past, perhaps searching for those ancient connections that we know exist, we are both losing touch with and imperiling the present. If we can combine our search with a renewed ecological consciousness, we won't need to spend the money and energy maintaining these unnatural "blandscapes" that extract such a high price.

I have hope that attitudes are changing, when I walk around my neighborhood and see here, a front lawn banished in favor of shrubs and groundcovers, and there, a planting of grasses and native perennials. In the U.S., the public continues to express a strong desire for a clean and healthy environment. According to a Decima Research survey, 75 per cent of Canadians feel that environmental problems affect their health and that of their families (1992), but the belief is not supported by action, such as recycling, gardening without chemicals or buying green products. Why is this? Because first, people aren't convinced they are at *personal* risk (yeah, it's a problem, but not *my* problem), and second, they feel that individually they cannot make a difference, that it's all beyond their control.[11] Not so. Every preventive action, however small, makes a difference. And the more such actions, the greater the ripple effect across all levels of society. The place where human culture and nature can find true balance is the garden. We do have the power.

Having ranted against lawns, I will now acknowledge that they are not going to go away in a hurry (not as long as people with sticks like to chase little white balls around), and yes, they make a lovely play surface for children and croquet. But perhaps you can do with less lawn; consider replacing some of it with groundcovers or shrub plantings.

It's time to throw off the "blandscape" blinders and bring the diversity of life into your garden. You'll be amazed at how dynamic your landscape will become— with insect life, new plants popping up (brought by birds and other visitors) and other plants happily seeding themselves about, rewarding you with a richer, healthier and more restorative space.

If You Must Have Some Lawn, Please:

- Don't use chemical pesticides or high-nitrogen fertilizers. They will merely kill off beneficial creatures in the soil, reduce fertility, pollute the groundwater and make your grass drug-dependent. Spray applications drift even on windless days, losing up to 80 per cent by dispersal. Exposure doesn't end at the lawn: up to 3 per cent of the pesticide may be tracked into homes on the feet of people walking over the lawn.[12] (See Chapter 7 for more on pesticides and fertilizers.)
- Worry less about "weeds": clover (*Trifolium*), for instance, stays green and fixes nitrogen in the soil. Spot-treat weeds rather than take the blanket approach: pull out what you can by hand and prevent them from going to seed.
- Set your lawnmower high and keep your grass about three inches (7.5 cm) long. It will withstand drought and pests better, have stronger roots, and shade out undesirables.
- Leave your grass clippings on the lawn (use a reel or mulching mower). They will break down and return nutrients to the soil.
- Top dress with compost or well-rotted manure at least once a year.
- The usual advice is to water deeply but less often, on the theory that frequent, shallow watering leads to shallow roots and weaker grass plants. But the result of field tests by Dr. Joe Vargas at Michigan State University flies in the face of this traditional wisdom. He found that 1/8 inch (3.2 mm) of water applied at the hottest part of the day actually benefited the grass more. The spray cooled the air making for more efficient photosynthesis, keeping the grass nice and green. There was no evidence that roots grew any shallower or were weaker with this treatment.[13]
- Don't attempt to grow grass in really unsuitable sites such as under heavy shade trees or on slopes. It won't thrive and you will spend an inordinate amount of time and energy getting frustrated. This is definitely not healthy for you or your garden.

6

WILD BY NATURE

Something that has long kept our cultigens and even our peopled landscapes healthy and tolerable is now disappearing. That valuable entity is wildness. If it is lost from the world around us, we will lose something within ourselves as well.

GARY NABHAN

Gardens by definition are tended and have always combined the natural with the artificial, with the human retaining (or attempting to retain) the upper hand. But, as more land is built on, covered by asphalt, farmed almost to death or clearcut, it is time for the balance to change. Our gardens need to become sanctuaries, places of restoration where we can allow nature freedom to work some magic. Let's call it finding the spirit of the place. Interpretive horticulturist Henry Kock says, "The more you do right, the stronger the spirit of the place will be."

So how do we find this spirit of place? How do we determine what is truly natural? It is difficult when our environment has undergone so many changes. It's like restoring a house built in 1810, with numerous additions and renovations in the interim. Do you put it back to the way it was when it was built, or to its handsome 1845 state or, perhaps, 1900? How do you decide what to preserve, what to throw away?

Several thousand years ago, my garden was under what is now Lake Ontario. Subsequently, it was forested, though much was cleared as the settlement around the mouth of the Credit River expanded. More recently, it was a market garden and a neighbor has told me of hopping the fence and pinching apples when she was a child. Now there are large trees—maples, oak, spruce, and remnants of the Carolinian forest such as tulip trees and sassafras—but just to the north lie sweeps of stubbled farmland with a few islands of forest, and much of that land is being eaten up by suburban sprawl. There are also patches of grassland, as well as wetlands along the Credit River and its tributaries.

Look about you and take your cue from what you see. Remember your garden is just one part of the whole, and if you create a totally alien landscape, you will lose the vitality and energy that comes from being connected with the larger world. Study the topography of your land, what it offers as far as soil, water, wind and sun, and existing vegetation. How can you enhance it to bring it teeming to life?

Someone with the 1810 house may decide to restore the garden as it was at that time, which can be a rewarding project. But you don't need to be (and often can't be) historically correct. And when you are looking at naturalizing your garden, it doesn't have to be every square inch. If a crowd of flamboyant canna lilies (*Canna*) stirs your soul, then by all means have them. But keep them in the more closely tended areas near the house and give nature freer rein beyond. I find the more natural the garden becomes, the more out of place exotic plants or even some common ones appear. I have walked around with a resplendent shrimp-colored annual geranium (*Pelargonium*) in hand and not found one spot where it fits in.

Naturalization

Naturalization is the effort to convert managed landscapes to more natural and naturally evolving landscapes in harmony with the surrounding bioregion and relatively free of long-term human intervention. It's easy to see naturalization's many benefits, compared to the traditional urban/suburban landscape. A naturalized landscape is dynamic in its diversity and processes, is less susceptible to disease and predation, makes minimal use of water and requires less management, i.e., human labor. If that weren't enough, it also attracts and supports wildlife, links with the larger environment, costs comparatively little to maintain and becomes a vital place for living and learning.

Naturalizing and finding the spirit of place involves seeking out plants native to the area. That sounds simple enough, but what exactly is meant by native plants? The term, native, usually applies to plants that were here before European

Some Natural Choices

Instead of	Plant
Norway maple (*Acer platanoides*), which shades out underplanting	Sugar maple (*A. saccharum*) and red maple (*A. rubrum*), which allow growth of rich understory
European highbush cranberry (*Viburnum opulus*)	Nannyberry (*Viburnum lantago*)
Rosa multiflora	Nutka rose (*Rosa nutkana*)
Oriental bittersweet (*Celastrus orbiculatus*)	American bittersweet (*Celastrus scandens*)
Japanese honeysuckle (*Lonicera japonica*)	Trumpet honeysuckle (*Lonicera sempervirens*)
Tatarian honeysuckle (*Lonicera tatarica*)	Black twinberry (*Lonicera involucrata*)
Gooseneck loosestrife (*Lysimachia clethroides*)	Culver's root (*Veronicastrum virginicum*)
Purple loosestrife (*Lythrum salicaria*)	Turtlehead (*Chelone*)
Japanese spurge (*Pachysandra terminalis*)	Allegheny spurge (*Pachysandra procumbens*) (Native woodlander with handsome toothed leaves and fragrant white flowers)

Blue-flowered Omphalodes cappadocica *and cream-splashed* Pulmonaria *are two well-behaved exotics, but periwinkle (Vinca minor) with its dark glossy green leaves has escaped the garden and become a problem, invading forests in a number of provinces.*

settlement, growing in all the ecosystems across North America from woodlands to tallgrass prairies. The settlers brought plants and seeds with them and carried them intentionally and unintentionally from place to place. Many of these introduced plants (also called *exotics*) such as Queen Anne's lace (*Anthriscus sylvestris*), chicory (*Cichorium*), and daylilies (*Hemerocallis*) have naturalized—become so widespread they are often regarded as native. They have adapted and fit quite beneficially into existing ecosystems.

Then there are the purple loosestrifes (*Lythrum salicaria*) and kudzus (*Pueraria lobata*) of this world, which reproduce quickly, adapt to just about anything, displace native species and resist efforts to eradicate them (more on those later). Just to confuse the issue, not all natives are content to live in polite co-existence, either. Wild grape (*Vitis*), blackberry (*Rubus*), poison ivy (*Toxicodendron*), wild onion (*Allium*) and cattail (*Typha*) are among the small number of native plants that are rambunctious to the point of invasiveness. The flora-rich United States counts just over 16,000 native plants and estimates that 4,000 exotic species have taken up residence, of which 400 are considered aggressively invasive.[1] The Canadian Botanical Conservation Network reports 3,200 species native to Canada and 800 aliens living outside cultivation.[2]

Many gardeners are plantaholics (guilty as charged) and crave the new, the different—in short, the exotic. Nurseries carry plants from all over the world, peonies (*Paeonia*) from China, arisaemas (*Arisaema*) from the Himalayas, flaxes (*Phormium*) from New Zealand, and sedums (*Sedum*) from Siberia. Are there places for these in our gardens? Some would say no. But often, closely related plant species exist naturally in different parts of the world, but in similar habitats. For instance, the tulip tree (*Liriodendron chinense*) of central China is virtually identical to the tulip tree (*L. tulipifera*) in North America's deciduous forest. Other global relatives include the birch (*Betula*), maple (*Acer*) and aster (*Aster*) species. Many exotics will be well-behaved in the garden such as hostas (*Hosta*) and pulmonarias (*Pulmonaria*), for instance, or a minor nuisance, such as the middle-aged spread of lambs' ears (*Stachys*). Even so, do some homework before introducing them into local ecosystems—what is restrained in one part of the country could be invasive elsewhere.

Native plants are desirable because they have evolved in biodiverse communities; they are tougher and more resistant to pest, disease and other stresses, and they draw wildlife. All true. But native plants will fare no better than exotics if the local environment has changed dramatically. Often, in urban settings, so little remains of the original topology, soil, water supply, etc., that any plant will be starting from scratch. So, it isn't an either–or situation. Better to choose a diverse mix of plants (native and exotic) that best suit the site. If they are happy, they will thrive and form an exuberant, close-knit community with all the attendant benefits—for you and the environment.

Native Plant Tips

- Buy plants that have been grown locally, rather than shipped in from farflung places.
- Buy from a reputable nursery that guarantees the plants are nursery-propagated, not collected from the wild.
- Never take plants from the wild yourself. Many native plants such as the small white lady's slipper (*Cypripedium candidum*) have a tenuous enough hold in the wild without being decimated by collectors. Others, such as trilliums (*Trillium*), frequently don't survive the attempted transplant.

- Do, however, rescue native plants if you know the site is slated for development and they will be destroyed. Make sure you have permission to take the plants.

Of Weeds and Wildflowers

One person's wildflower is another person's weed and vice versa. Usually, when people talk of wildflower gardens, they are referring to meadows, which have become quite popular with their lure of carefree looks and easy maintenance. But sore disappointment awaits the deluded soul who thinks they can grab one of those "meadows-in-a-can" and skip about like Johnny or Johanna Appleseed, then sit back and *voilà,* a field of wildflowers is born. They probably will be no more gratified if they decide just to let the grassy areas go and see what comes up, since it's unlikely that many native plants or seeds remain there.

Like any naturalized garden, a meadow requires careful consideration of existing conditions, decisions about the type of plant community and thorough site preparation. The model to look to is wild prairie, but sadly precious little of that is still around. For instance, less than 1 per cent of the tallgrass prairie that once covered 400,000 square miles from Canada to Texas remains, remembered only in place names such as Prairie Siding and Raleigh Plains. We may think of prairies as expanses of monotony; in fact, the prairie landscape was remarkably diverse. Within the three main types (tallgrass, mixed-grass and shortgrass) were hundreds of different grasses and herbaceous flowering plants called *forbs.*

There's also far more to prairie than meets the eye—as much as 75 per cent of the total biomass is underground (quite the opposite of forests). Prairie plants send extensive root systems as deep as 15 feet (4.5 m) into the soil. And it is a tremendously efficient ecosystem, combining cool- and warm-season grasses and drought-tolerant forbs in non-competitive

A Grass Sampler

Your personal prairie can begin with grasses such as:
- Big bluestem (*Andropogon gerardii*): The defining grass of the tallgrass prairie, it grows 7 feet (2.1 m) or taller. It's also called turkey foot after the shape of its seed heads and was used by native peoples to treat digestive problems.
- Little bluestem (*Andropogon scoparius*): Reaching just 3 to 4 feet (90 cm to 120 cm), it turns a glorious bronze-orange after a frost and holds its fluffy seed heads most decoratively.
- Cord grass (*Spartina pectinata*): A moisture-loving tallgrass, with stout stems reaching 10 feet (3 m) in height and leaves up to 4 feet (1.2 m) long, it was traditionally used for thatched roofs and as a fuel.
- Indian grass (*Sorghastrum nutans*): Reaching 6 feet (1.8 m), this puts the amber in amber waves, with its golden seed heads and bronze leaves in fall.
- Blue grama grass (*Bouteloua gracilis*): Named for the Spanish writer, Claudio Boutelou (1774-1842), this short tufted grass (1 to 2 feet/30 to 60 cm) has a distinctive seed head that looks like one or two eyebrows on short stalks.

co-existence. With much of the top growth and about 50 per cent of the root systems dying back every year, there is very tight nutrient recycling. The steady accumulation of organic matter leads to incredibly rich deep dark soil, the richest in the world, which is why the prairies were so quickly plowed under to be replaced by monocultures of wheat, corn, barley and rye. (And, of course, the thousands of insects and animals such as buffalo, prairie dogs and black-footed ferrets, all parts of the prairie ecosystem, were also banished.)

Bees (and butterflies) adore purple coneflower (Echinacea purpurea), *a wonderful plant for prairie, meadow or any home garden.*

A prairie garden is not an overnight thing, however. It requires good planning and close attention for the initial couple of years anyway. First and foremost is good site preparation—making sure your wild seedlings have a clean, weed-free bed to start with. The site can be planted with plugs (small seedlings) or sown with seeds. Because the ground is freshly prepared and open, weeds will present a real challenge. A straw mulch can help, as can a "nurse crop" of annual flax or oats or rye (but avoid grain or perennial rye). Cut or mow weeds rather than pull them. The traditional maintenance method of a prairie was fire, set by lightning or native peoples. Periodic burning stimulates growth by reducing competition from weeds and woody plants, and returning nutrients to the soil through the ash. If burning isn't an option, mow instead.

Some Favorite Forbs

Wild bergamot (*Monarda fistulosa*)

Black-eyed Susan (*Rudbeckia hirta*)

Brown-eyed Susan (*Rudbeckia triloba*)

Compass plant (*Silphium laciniatum*)

New England aster (*Aster novae-angliae*)

Ox-eye sunflower (*Heliopsis helianthoides*)

Partridge pea (*Cassia fasciculata*)

Purple coneflower (*Echinacea purpurea*)

Rattlesnake master (*Eryngium yuccifolium*)

Stiff goldenrod (*Solidago rigida*)

Tall ironweed (*Vernonia altissima*)

Meadows don't come in cans. They need good planning and careful site preparation.

Remember that the cultivated versions of some of these plants that are available in garden centers may not adapt as readily as their wild parents and may not be as attractive to bees and butterflies, since they have been bred for specific characteristics to make them more "garden-worthy."

When is a wildflower a weed? Many wildflowers have "weed" as part of their common name (ironweed, joe pye weed, jewelweed and milkweed), but, for the prairie or wildlife gardener, they aren't weeds at all. Weed may be just another pejorative term humans have devised for plants that have valid roles to play, but just don't happen to figure in our horticultural drama. Queen Anne's lace (*Anthriscus sylvestris*), for instance is definitely weedy, but is a magnet for insects, while milkweed (*Asclepias*) is the host plant for monarch butterflies (an endangered species in Canada). For many gardeners, a weed is a plant growing where it isn't wanted—from dandelions in the lawn to self-seeded cosmos. Ecologically, a weed is a plant that is highly adaptable, produces lots of seeds which disperse rapidly and germinate easily and can dominate a variety of habitats.

Weeds are opportunistic creatures, rushing in to fill any patch of bare soil, which is why you see so many along roadsides, in ditches and on abandoned lots. Often they are the first settlers in the process known as *succession*. Their roots go deep and bring up nutrients from far below. As they grow and die back, they enrich the soil, making it easier for larger plants, grasses and shrubs to move in. Over time, rapid-growing, sun-loving trees take the stage, acting as nurses to larger trees which will eventually shade them out in turn. When a system matures in complexity and stays relatively stable, it is called a *climax situation*.

However, when there is an interruption—when the forest is cut down or devastated by fire, or when roads are pushed through—the weeds are just waiting in the wings. Fireweed (*Epilobium angustifolium*) is named for the speed with which it appears after a forest fire; its rapid growth stabilizes the soil and ultimately aids the land's healing. Annual weeds rush in to colonize disturbed soil, while perennial weeds thrive in fertile soils. As we turn over our planting beds, and lavish compost on our green beauties, we are creating a weed's Promised Land. What you do about them depends on the kind of garden you have and the sort of gardener you are. If you change your mind about what you regard as a weed, you'll have got rid of a lot of them without lifting a finger! (For more on weed control, see Chapter 7).

Usually merely a nuisance in the home garden, weeds on grazing lands can poison livestock, and some weeds, including woody plants, are highly invasive. Some of the worst offenders are: purple loosestrife (*Lythrum salicaria*), leafy spurge (*Euphorbia esula*), garlic mustard (*Alliaria petiolata*), Japanese knotweed (*Polygonum cuspidatum*), common and glossy buckthorn (*Rhamnus cathartica* and *R. frangula*), autumn olive (*Elaeagnus umbellata*), dog-strangling vine (*Cynanchum rossicum* and *C. medium*) knapweeds (*Centaurea* spp.), Canada thistle (*Cirsium arvense*), Dalmatian toadflax (*Linaria dalmatica*) and Oriental bittersweet (*Celastrus orbiculatus*). These plants are rampaging through woods, rivers and meadows, displacing native species and disrupting ecosystems. If you have any of these, oust them if you can.

Many plants commonly sold in nurseries can be invasive: look for the words, "vigorous," "aggressive," "indefinite spread," and similar euphemisms. Think twice, no, make that three times, before planting them,

The Good Side of Weeds

Weeds attract beneficial insects. Contrary to the often repeated opinion that weeds harbor harmful pests, studies show that, in fact, they sustain the predators that will reduce crop damage. Apple orchards with weedy wildflowers have greater rates of parasitism of tent caterpillars and codling moths compared to weed-free orchards.

Weeds also draw birds, butterflies and pollinating bees: goldfinches like dandelion seeds, while many birds snack on teasel (*Dipsacus*), thistles (*Cirsium*), shepherd's purse (*Capsella bursa-pastoris*) and chickweed (*Stellaria*). Butterflies love thistles and bees adore clover (*Trifolium*).

Weeds enrich the soil—leguminous weeds, such as clovers, fix nitrogen, for example. Even if you pull your weeds, put them on your compost pile. Nettles (*Urtica dioica*), rich in iron and nitrogen, and comfrey (*Symphytum*), full of nitrogen, potassium and potash, are two of the best compost activators. Dandelions (*Taraxacum*) contain iron, potash and phosphate, while yarrow (*Achillea*) has these plus nitrogen. And over winter, weeds can prevent erosion and leaching.

If you succumb to variegated goutweed's green-and-white charms, make sure you confine it to where it can't spread or, better yet, keep it in a pot.

or confine them to containers. I'm thinking of goutweed (*Aegopodium podagraria*), which I have spent 12 years trying to get rid of; gardener's garters (*Phalaris arundinacea*); lemon balm (*Melissa officinalis*); lily of the valley (*Convallaria*); mints (*Mentha* spp.) and many loosestrifes (*Lysimachia* spp).

Poisonous Plants

We eat plants all the time, but some of them can kill you or cause severe stomach aches, vomiting and irregular heartbeats among other symptoms. The plants are not out to do you in—they are seeking to protect themselves from predation. We harness their toxins in such biopesticides as pyrethrin and rotenone. And scientists now believe that plant-produced cyanide could be effective against cancer. It is often a question of degree: a little can be beneficial; a lot can be harmful.

The role of plant toxins reaches even further into nature's intricately woven web. For example, the monarch butterfly dines on poisonous milkweed with impunity, absorbing the toxins that then render it unpalatable to birds. In another remarkable adaptation, the viceroy butterfly "borrows" the unpalatability defense by mimicking the monarch's appearance so closely that birds regard it with equal distaste.

The natural landscape is full of such fascinating relationships as plants and animals evolve and adapt as part of nature's constant pursuit of balance. By understanding these processes and taking a holistic approach in our gardens, we can renew our connections with the past and restore the spirits of place.

What to Do If Poisoning Is Suspected

- Encourage the person to drink a glassful of water or diluted clear juice, provided that he or she is fully conscious and in no apparent pain. Then dial 911.
- If you go to hospital, take a good-sized piece of the plant with you with leaves, flowers or berries, and write down the name of the plant if you know it.

- For pets, remove any plant material from the animal's mouth, rinse the mouth area and see if the animal will drink a small amount of water. Watch for excessive or foamy salivation. Don't try to induce vomiting. Call your veterinarian or emergency clinic and take your pet in, along with samples of the plant's leaves, fruit and flowers.

Beware of These Plants

There are many plants that you should beware of, especially if you have young children or pets.

Plant	Toxic Parts
Hyacinth (*Hyacinthus*), daffodil (*Narcissus*)	Bulbs
Oleander (*Nerium oleander*)	Leaves, branches
Castor bean (*Ricinus communis*)	Seeds
Monkshood (*Aconitum*)	Whole plant
Lily of the valley (*Convallaria*)	Leaves, flowers
Foxglove (*Digitalis*)	All parts
Rhubarb (*Rheum*)	Leaves
Daphne (*Daphne*)	All parts, especially berries
Horse chestnut (*Aesculus hippocastanum*)	Flowers, leaves, fruit
Wisteria (*Wisteria*)	All parts, especially seeds
Laurels (*Kalmia*), rhodos, azaleas (*Rhododendron*)	All parts
Yew (*Taxus*)	Berries, foliage
Cherries (*Prunus*)	Twigs, foliage
Baneberry (*Actaea*)	Berries, root, sap
Elderberry (*Sambucus canadensis*)	All parts, especially roots
Black nightshade (*Solanum nigrum*)	All parts (The huckleberry, *Solanum melanocerasum*, is the one with edible fruit used in pies, jams, etc.)
Potato (*Solanum tuberosum*)	Green potatoes can be fatal; store them in the dark
Poison hemlock (*Conium maculatum*)	All parts (looks like a wild carrot)
Water hemlock (*Cicuta maculata*)	All parts
Jimson weed (*Datura*)	All parts[3]

7

GROWING ORGANICALLY

Everything that grows is food for something else. Innumerable hosts of predators, both animal and vegetable, are constantly at work, not only on our precious plants but on each other. The best any gardener can do is to referee the performance with a bias in favor of our side.

HUGH JOHNSON,
THE PRINCIPLES OF GARDENING

The word *organic* is very elastic, stretching to apply to everything from apples and olive oil to inks, diapers, shampoo and cotton underwear. It can simply mean something "derived from living organisms" or merely "healthful and close to nature." But in a food and gardening context, it means one thing: "growing without the use of synthetic pesticides, herbicides or fertilizers." To take it one step further, it also means, "to fit into nature's systems and preserve their integrity."

As we've seen in earlier chapters, the effects of chemicals on soil, water, plants and animals, indeed all the living things our lives depend on, are grievous and far-ranging. The litany of death and destruction continues, from grotesquely deformed frogs as wetlands are permeated with lethal runoff, to thousands of migratory birds killed in Florida by *fenthion*, a widely banned pesticide still sprayed to kill mosquitoes[1]; from poisoned bees, our most valuable pollinators, to fish and crustaceans wiped out by toxic pollution of rivers and lakes.

Human health is equally affected, both directly and indirectly. Our bodies now harbor chemicals that didn't even exist 60 years ago, and exposure to these substances has been implicated in leukemia, liver impairment, genetic damage, allergies, asthma, fibromyalgia, and decreased fertility.[2] Yet North Americans are still spending billions of dollars a year on insecticides, herbicides and fungicides.

There's no denying that nature produces its share of toxic substances: many plants and animals have sophisticated forms of chemical weapons, both offensive and defensive. But they are very specific: a venomous snake attacks only certain creatures and relatively few of them. Castor bean plants poison only those foolish enough to eat the seeds. Since the invention of DDT just before the Second World War, human science has concocted a chemical arsenal largely composed of "broad spectrum" or non-selective pesticides such as carbaryl, malathion and diazinon. Not only do these wipe out every living thing that happens to be near the "target," but they also don't readily biodegrade, and consequently contaminate groundwater and the soil. "Selective" pesticides, targeted at a specific pest, may not be toxic to mammals, but can still be lethal to fish or bees. Toxins move up the food chain as bird eats bug, ferret eats bird, coyote eats ferret, etc., becoming ever more concentrated. And, once released into the environment, these contaminants don't stay put. Wind, water runoff, rain, sea currents and animals can carry them thousands of miles. Traces of insecticides used in the tropics have been detected in trees in the Arctic, while pesticides never used in the North have been found in the tissues of polar bears.[3]

Synergy comes into play here, too, because an unknown, and possibly greater, hazard is the synergistic effects of the chemical stew to which we (and the earth) are being exposed—how one pesticide may interact with another, how a chemical will break down in the body, how all the so-called "inert" substances which carry the active ingredients might interact. In fact, those "inert" carriers which are not listed on labels include such things as cadmium and asbestos fibers, hazardous on their own.

Yes, there are diseases and predations we want to protect our plants from, but reaching for a toxic chemical is not the simple solution you might think. As Daar and the Olkowskis point out, it's like kicking a malfunctioning TV; with luck, you might jar it into working, for a while, but it is no permanent solution.[4] It ultimately doesn't work because first, it kills the pest's predators, too, and the pest population is likely to rebound more quickly than the predators, so soon you are back where you started; and second, more pests are becoming resistant to

What You Can Do: Preventive Measures

- Grow a diverse (there's that word again) mix of flowering and fruiting plants and keep them as vigorous as possible. Stressed, weak or ailing plants send a chemical come-hither message to pests.
- Choose disease-resistant species or cultivars, and native plants.
- Mulch, mulch, mulch and grow healthy soil (see Chapter 2). The richer the soil is in organic matter, the more disease-suppressing microorganisms there are.
- Nothing beats the mano-a-mano method of hand-picking (and foot-stomping) pests. Going around at night with a flashlight will reveal the most destructive culprits.
- Devise traps (beer in a pan for slugs, for example) and barriers (to foil cutworms and other munchers, remove the bottom from a plastic container and push the container around the plant, or place a twig alongside its stem). Protect veggies with floating row covers—thin fabric "blankets" that let in light and water but prevent flying insects from laying their eggs on the plants.

Barriers such as plastic containers with their bottoms cut out protect young plants from greedy predators.

Not only are spiders the most valuable predators in our gardens, they also weave the most exquisite embroideries out of silk and light.

pesticides (about 450 insects are now known to be resistant compared to fewer than 10 in the 1950s).[5]

Instead, remember what Yogi Berra said, "You can observe a lot by watching." Observe what is happening (the when, where, and what), understand the concepts at work (the why and the how), learn what tactics have been used elsewhere, and then and only then determine what steps to take. Rather than slapping on Band-Aid solutions, we need to look at maintaining the health of the system as a whole. I call it holistic preventive medicine.

Good Guys to the Rescue

It may not seem like it when your roses are being demolished, but probably 99 per cent of the bugs and insects in your garden are beneficial in some way. The *good guys* are basically guzzlers, suckers and zappers. Guzzlers such as ladybugs (or more correctly lady beetles) and ground beetles devour their victims; suckers such as assassin bugs, lacewing larvae and hover fly larvae pierce their prey and suck it dry; while zappers (the little parasitoid wasps) lay their eggs on or in the host, which provides the newly hatched larvae with their baby food—giving new meaning to the phrase *eating out.*

Spiders They may speak to our primal fears, but spiders are the most valuable predators in our gardens. Maybe because there are so many of them—one estimate put the number of spiders in an acre of undisturbed English meadow at over 2.2 million. Even if we don't have close to that, they are out there devouring caterpillars, leafhoppers, gypsy moths, aphids and much else. Their ravening appetites aside, I want spiders in my garden just to see their silken air embroideries catch the dew and the morning light.

Lady Beetle The lady beetle is a voracious aphid-hunter, as are its larvae, described as tiny black "alligators" with colored markings. The one we know best is the convergent lady beetle, which is orange-red variously spotted with black (the aptly named twice-stabbed lady beetle is black with two red spots). I don't recommend buying packages of lady beetles from stores or mail order. They have likely been collected in a hibernating state, some die en route and the survivors are far more likely to fly away than feed on your pests.

Ground and Rove Beetles Those big, black or brown beetles with an iridescent sheen that scuttle through fallen leaves are ground beetles. They devour mites, snails, weevils and slugs, and some even climb trees and eat caterpillars. Unfortunately, they also eat earthworms, but one hopes not too many. Rove beetles, which live under stones and in mulch, have a similar diet, though one of them, called the *devil's coachman*, has a distinct preference for brown garden snails.

Lacewings Delicately skimming the air, green lacewings are entrancing with their diaphanous, veined wings and golden eyes. They're just after pollen and honeydew, however. It is their less beauteous, alligator-like larvae that have a healthy taste for aphids, scales, mealybugs, whiteflies, leafhoppers, thrips and others.

Hover Flies They look like mini-wasps and feed on pollen as well as aphids, caterpillars, beetles, thrips and sawfly larvae. Their own larvae are aphid-killers *par excellence.* Hover flies are particularly susceptible to insecticides.

The Real Bugs In the bug-eat-bug world, there are assassin bugs, pirate bugs, spined soldier bugs and big-eyed bugs, to name a few. They are unfussy eaters, downing spider mites, caterpillars, thrips, insect eggs and much else with relish.

The good guys like a supply of pollen and nectar in case the pest supply runs low. You can attract them by growing: Alfalfa (*Medicago*), coneflowers (*Echinacea*), coriander (*Coriandrum sativum*), cosmos (*Cosmos*), daisies (*Aster*), fennel (*Foeniculum*), goldenrod (*Solidago*), Queen Anne's lace (*Anthriscus sylvestris*), spearmint (*Mentha*), salvia (*Salvia*), sweet alyssum (*Lobularia maritima*), thyme (*Thymus*), tickseed (*Coreopsis*) and yarrow (*Achillea*). They also appreciate something to wash it down with, so fill a shallow container with water and an "island" of rocks.

Less Toxic Pesticides

If you must resort to pesticides, choose the least toxic and most specific to that particular pest. Avoid spreading it far and wide, and follow safety precautions.

Build a Toad Abode

Break a semi-circle out of the rim of an eight-inch (20 cm) clay pot, then place it upside down in a shady, out-of-the-way spot, preferably near water. He (or she) will thank you by eating 10,000 slugs, sowbugs, cutworms, earwigs and the like in just one season.

- **Bt** is a bacterial pesticide containing *Bacillus thuringiensis* and used against caterpillars, beetle larvae and flies. A stomach poison, it must be ingested by the pest, but is safe for other species. Other microbial pesticides harness fungi, viruses and nematodes in fighting insects and weeds. Much work is being done to develop safer "biopesticides" building on nature's own systems; for instance, isoflavonoids derived from soybeans and peas can effectively combat fungal pathogens.
- **Diatomaceous earth** is a silica dust that desiccates the insect's skin; it's used against slugs and snails, as well as wasps, ticks and cockroaches.
- **Insecticidal soap** contains fatty acids which penetrate the skin and cause the cells to collapse. It's used against soft-bodied insects such as aphids and whiteflies, and doesn't harm mammals. It also biodegrades rapidly in the soil.
- **Horticultural oils** smother insects or overwintering eggs on trees and shrubs as well as perennials; they're used against scales, caterpillars, leafminers, mites, sawflies, beetles and whiteflies.
- **Pyrethrin**, derived from chrysanthemum flowers, disrupts insects' nerve impulses causing paralysis. Used against many garden insects, it's relatively safe for mammals but can be toxic to cats. Pyrethroids are synthetic versions of pyrethrin. (Interestingly, pests develop greater resistance to the synthetic pyrethroid than to natural pyrethrin.)

Do It Yourself

There's a wealth of recipes for homemade sprays in organic gardening books and web sites, including baking soda spray to treat anthracnose, leaf blight and powdery mildew; chive spray for apple scab and downy mildew on cucumber, pumpkin and zucchini; horseradish spray as a general disease preventative and garlic sprays against fungus and mildews. A caution: garlic oil is a broad-spectrum pesticide and can kill beneficial insects, so use selectively. Growing garlic around disease-prone plants is safer. Experiment with small quantities of these sprays in a small area first to be sure they don't damage the plant, and never spray in full hot sun.

Epsom Salts

A quick picker-upper of tomatoes, roses and peppers, Epsom salts is a good source of magnesium, which strengthens cell walls and boosts production of chlorophyll, fruit and nuts. A deficiency shows up in yellowing, curling leaves, retarded growth and sour fruit. Although you can scratch Epsom salts into the soil, the best method is as a foliar feed: dissolve 1 tablespoon (15 mL) of Epsom salts per gallon (3.8 L) of water, and spray roses in spring and at flowering. Spray tomatoes and peppers at transplanting, first flowering and fruit set.[6]

Milk for Mildew

Powdery mildew can be controlled by a spray consisting of one part milk to nine parts water. Even plain water works: giving rose bushes a good bath every three days washes off the spores and coats the leaves with a film of water that prevents additional spores from germinating.

Fertilizers

Nurturing souls that we are, we want to feed our plants to make them bigger, more floriferous or higher yielding. Unfortunately, chemical fertilizers with their high nitrogen cause more problems than they solve. Nitrogen is an essential element for plants, but too much of it causes rapid tender growth that draws insects like guests to a wedding banquet. It also disrupts the cozy and complex affair that the plant's roots carry on with nutrient-bearing mycorrhizal fungi (see Chapter 2), and shuts down the natural nitrogen-fixing bacteria. Having damaged the soil, excess nitrogen then washes out into streams and lakes, destroying the balance there, too.

The best fertilizers are organic matter such as well-rotted animal manure, green manure (a quick-growing crop such as winter rye that is turned into the soil), seaweed, fish meal, leaf mold and compost. These break down slowly, release nitrogen very gradually, and encourage the soil's microbial life, leading to steady strong plant growth. If you do buy fertilizer (marked organic or not), check the listing of nitrogen (N), phosphorus (P) and potassium (K) on the bag. If the NPK listing (20-20-20, for example) adds up to more than 15, or if one number is higher than eight, it is probably chemical.

Weed Wise

No garden can be or should be free of weeds, which do have their good sides (see Chapter 6). Give a plant a second thought before tagging it "weed." Once you have, though:

- Remove weeds before they set seed, and toss them in your compost pile.
- Weed after a rain—they'll uproot more easily.
- Pour boiling water on weeds or grass growing through pavers or patio stones. Don't use salt; it's not good for the soil inhabitants.
- Try to get out all of tap-rooted weeds such as garlic mustard (*Alliaria petiolata*). Any scrap of root left will resprout.
- Hoe weeds out when small, cutting them just below the surface.
- Don't turn over the soil; it just brings more weed seeds to the top.
- If you can't beat 'em, eat 'em (see Chapter 10 for edible weeds).
- Plant densely and mulch well.
- Relax and see the beauty of the garden first, the weeds second.

Toss kitchen scraps, leaves, weeds without seeds, etc., in a bin with a bit of soil and water; fluff it occasionally and black gold will be yours.

Black Gold

Compost is called *black gold* because it's so valuable to the garden and no one ever has enough of it. Technically, it's partially decayed organic matter that's added to the soil to enrich it and increase its humus content. Needless to say, plants love it, or rather the fertile soil life it stimulates. And there's more: Ohio State University researchers have found that the microbes in compost can switch on the plant's biochemical defenses against disease.[7]

There's been a whole lot written about making compost—the right containers, activators, carbon-nitrogen ratios, etc.—but really it's a simple process. Just throw any kind of plant material (grass clippings, kitchen scraps, leaves, weeds without seeds, sawdust), wet and dry, into a pile, adding a bit of soil here and there, and keep it moist but not soggy. (Don't put meat, dairy products, fat or pet wastes into it.) Stir and fluff it occasionally and let it quietly rot down. Two great compost additives are nettles (*Urtica dioica*) because of their high nitrogen, and comfrey (*Symphytum*) with its many nutrients, especially potash. The pile (or container if you use one) should be at least one cubic yard in size for the compost to really get cooking. In six months or so, you should strike it rich with your own black gold—and feel good about all the material you have diverted from a landfill.

Tea Time

Compost tea and manure tea are valuable fertilizers, foliar feeds, and disease preventatives. The usual recipe calls for soaking a bag of compost or manure in a barrel or garbage can of water for a few days, removing the bag and using the resulting tea. However, soil scientist Elaine Ingham suggests using loose compost (or manure), a five-gallon bucket, plus a small pump and three bubblers to oxygenate the brew, and letting it infuse for just two or three days. Aerating it keeps the microorganisms alive and kicking and makes the tea more effective.[8] Many organic gardeners also swear by comfrey (*Symphytum*), chamomile (*Chamaemelum*), horsetail (*Equisetum*) and stinging nettle (*Urtica dioica*) teas.

Drawing a Wild Crowd

Attracting birds, bees, butterflies, toads, bats and other creatures will provide not only pest control and improved pollination but also music, animation and endless fascination. Their needs are simple: food, water and lodging.

The principal providers of food and shelter are trees and shrubs, especially if grown as a community or an edge planting (see Chapter 5). Grouping shrubs, ground-covering perennials and grasses around trees—think thickets—provides a multi-level habitat. Dead trees are valuable "apartment houses" for more than 400 species of birds, mammals and amphibians, so leave them if you can. Evergreens offer year-round safe shelter, while a careful selection of fruit- and nut-bearing woody plants will provide food for all seasons. Native species (see Chapter 6) are desirable because they're part of the critters' familiar domain.

Vines are also valuable cover, food and nesting places: try trumpet honeysuckle (*Lonicera sempervirens*), Virginia creeper (*Parthenocissus*), native American bittersweet (*Celastrus scandens*), and climbing hydrangea (*Hydrangea petiolaris*), a favorite of robins in our garden, despite the fact that it's right beside the back door. (Real birdbrains, robins insist on nesting in such impossibly precarious places. I'm surprised any babies survive. They won't nest in boxes, but you can build a shelf with sides on it that would provide a measure of security.)

Hummingbirds fuel their tiny bodies on nectar, zooming in on tubular flowers (particularly red and yellow ones) such as salvia (*Salvia*), cardinal flower (*Lobelia cardinalis*), honeysuckle (*Lonicera*), fuchsia (*Fuchsia*) and penstemon (*Penstemon*).

Birdhouses are also welcome (just make sure you fit the house to the potential tenants) and water is a must, whether it's a full-fledged pond and waterfall,

Trees and Shrubs for Birds

Conifers including cedar (*Thuja*), pine (*Pinus*), juniper (*Juniperus*), spruce (*Picea*)	Hollies, evergreen and deciduous (*Ilex*)
	Mulberry (*Morus*)
Cherry (*Prunus*)	Oak (*Quercus*)
Crabapple (*Malus*)	Serviceberry (*Amelanchier*)
Dogwood (*Cornus*)	Spicebush (*Lindera*)
Elder (*Sambucus*)	Viburnum (*Viburnum*)

a formal bird bath or simply an old basin. The key is to keep it clean of algae and replenish it often (see Chapter 3 for more on water features). Birds have a hard time "drinking" snow in winter—a submersible heating element in your pond or birdbath will keep it ice-free.

Some birds prefer open meadows to forests, so gardens of grasses and wildflowers will draw them, as well as many butterflies and insects. (See Chapter 6.)

Don't overtidy the garden; leave brush piles as hidey-holes and don't cut the seed heads off grasses and perennials though I confess I behead grasses such as northern sea oats (*Chasmanthium latifolium*) because they self-sow so vigorously.

Butterflies

You can't have butterflies without caterpillars. So you need to grow not just butterflies' favorite nectar-loaded flowers but also their larvae's baby food. Butterflies don't eat and run; they prefer to eat and lay their eggs close by, and they can be very picky. The caterpillars of the Eastern black swallowtail, for instance, will dine only on members of the carrot family (celery, dill, parsley, etc.), while monarch butterflies both feed and lay their eggs on milkweeds.

Deer generally avoid them, but birds love dogwoods, many of which boast gorgeous flowers, fruit and splendid fall color.

Unwelcome Visitors

Providing such a range of irresistible delights can bring less welcome visitors such as raccoons, skunks, rabbits, mice, woodchucks and deer. My husband would add squirrels to this list, but I don't mind them except when they tear the buds off my star magnolia and heads off my tulips, flinging them aside without so much as a bite. Depending on the amount of damage these animals cause in your garden you can try setting live traps, placing wire mesh around vulnerable plants, putting up fencing or growing their least-liked plants. Though really hungry deer will try anything, they generally avoid gray-leafed plants and those with aromatic foliage, as well as oaks (*Quercus*), maples (*Acer*), dogwoods (*Cornus*), euonymus (*Euonymus*), serviceberry (*Amelanchier*), holly (*Ilex*), Western red cedar (*Thuja plicata*), cinquefoil (*Potentilla*), many clematis (*Clematis*), irises (*Iris*), larkspur (*Consolida*), marigolds (*Tagetes*), candytuft (*Iberis*), yarrow (*Achillea*) and zinnias (*Zinnia*). Squirrels and mice will leave daffodils (*Narcissus*), allium (*Allium*) and fritillaria (*Fritillaria*) bulbs alone—interplanting these with your tulips will discourage those seeking a tulip snack.

Just as in the movie, *Field of Dreams*, "if you build it, they will come." And whether we consider them desirable or undesirable, the flora and fauna that come are only responding to natural cues and the need to survive. The label "undesirable" is often a subjective (human) one. In nature, an infestation of canker worms, for example, is a setback for the tree they defoliate but a surprise feast for a flock of passing birds. Such things are usually an imbalance that will be corrected in the course of time. So it makes sense in our own gardens to intervene as little as possible, and, if driven to action, to take a page from nature's book and follow those instructions as precisely as we can.

Plants for a Butterfly Garden

Nectar Plants	Larval Foods
Allium (*Allium*)	Milkweed (*Asclepias*)
Butterfly bush (*Buddleja*)	Poplar (*Populus*)
Milkweed (*Asclepias*)	Willows (*Salix*)
Stonecrop (*Sedum*)	Clover (*Trifolium*)
Lavender (*Lavandula*)	Nasturtiums (*Tropaeolum majus*)
Heliotrope (*Heliotropium*)	Nettles (*Urtica dioica*)
Bee balm (*Monarda*)	Anise (*Pimpinella*)
Blanket flower (*Gaillardia*)	Fennel (*Foeniculum*) and Dill (*Anethum graveolens*)
Tickseed (*Coreopsis*)	Pearly everlasting (*Anaphalis*)
Willows (*Salix*)	Violets (*Viola*)

8

GOOD EATING

Edible, adj. Good to eat,
and wholesome to digest,
as a worm to a toad,
a toad to a snake,
a snake to a pig,
a pig to a man,
and a man to
a worm.

AMBROSE BIERCE,
THE DEVIL'S DICTIONARY, 1911

Nowhere in the healing garden is there a more direct link between nature and our health than in the vegetable patch or orchard. There we cut out all the middle men, the anonymous pickers in distant fields, the packers, sorters, shippers and truckers who transport our food an average of 2,000 km.[1] We can just reach out and pluck a pea pod or sun-warmed tomato right off the vine, still coursing with life and packed with nutrients, and pop them in our mouths. The speedier sweet corn goes from stalk to cooking pot the better, or the sugars in each delicate kernel start converting to starch (Tip: cool is key. Plunge just-picked cobs into a bucket of ice water, and refrigerate them if you can't eat them right away.)

Time is the essence here. Once picked, fruit and vegetables start losing nutrients, especially sensitive ones such as vitamin C. For instance, potatoes lose as much as 70 per cent of their vitamin C content in just days, even when stored in ideal conditions. It's even worse with improper storage: kale stored at room temperature lost 60 per cent more vitamin C in two days than refrigerated kale.[2] Plus there is an earthy satisfaction in growing your own food from seed to harvest. It reaches deep into our ancestral roots. And you can experiment with weird and wonderful delectables your local supermarket has never seen.

Despite the blandishments of "burgers-coke-n-fries," we know very well that eating fresh fruit and vegetables is good for us: to maintain healthy bodies, boost our immune systems, ward off obesity and reduce the risk of disease. The dark green leafy veggies (the ones you disliked as a kid) are rich in calcium, magnesium, potassium and iron, as well as vitamins, a surprising amount of protein, and the F word—*fiber*. We now know that a B vitamin called *folic acid* (found in these same leafy vegetables as well as dried beans, citrus fruits and berries) helps prevent birth defects such as spina bifida.

Calcium-rich vegetables and herbs, such as parsley, dill, lettuce, tomato, rocket, onion and garlic, fight osteoporosis, the bane of aging female baby boomers, while a host of plant minerals and vitamins have been enlisted to battle cancer. Beta carotene (a provitamin A found in carrots, sweet potatoes, squash, pumpkin and apricots) maintains good vision, protects the cardiovascular system, strengthens immune functions and promotes wound healing.

This brings us to the wonderful world of *phytochemicals*. These are plant chemicals that may affect our health but are not counted as essential nutrients. As research scientist and microscopist Michael Davidson points out, plants developed these compounds first to survive in an "oxygen-polluted" atmosphere (hence the term, *antioxidants*) and then as defenses against bacteria, fungi, viruses and cell damage. When animals (including us) eat plants, they "borrow" some of these protective chemicals, which include:[3]

Allicin This sulfurous compound gives **garlic** and **onions** their pungent aroma. Long known as an antibacterial agent, it is now seen to lower bad cholesterol, protect against atherosclerosis and stroke and reduce the risk of cancer.

Butyl Phthalide The source of **celery's** distinctive taste and smell, it offers protection against cancer, high blood pressure and high cholesterol levels. (The ancient Greeks must have known something—they awarded their athletes with bunches of celery.)

Capsaicin This gives **chili peppers** their heat and the burning sensation in your mouth (or eyes should you touch them with pepper-tainted fingers), but it is also being used to prevent peptic ulcers (spicy is good after all), relieve headaches and arthritis pain, treat heart irregularities and fight cancer. Wow.

Ellagic Acid A natural pesticide in many fruits, such as **apples, strawberries, grapes** and **raspberries**, this phytochemical fights cancer in humans.

Isoflavones Found in **soy, peanuts, lentils** and other legumes, **grains** and **green tea**, isoflavones are phytoestrogens which can alleviate menopausal symptoms, reduce cholesterol levels and protect against heart disease, osteoporosis and some cancers.

Your own freshly picked vegetables and herbs don't just tantalize the taste buds, they are chock full of nutrients and health-enhancing phytochemicals.

Isoflavonoids and Indoles These potent cancer fighters are found in cruciferous vegetables (**brussels sprouts, mustard greens, broccoli, cabbage,** etc.).

Lutein An antioxidant found in leafy green vegetables, such as **spinach, kale, collard greens, romaine lettuce, leeks** and **peas**, lutein protects against age-related macular degeneration, the leading cause of blindness in people over 65. It's not just carrots that are good for your eyes.

Top 10 Cancer Fighters

1. Broccoli
2. Tomatoes
3. Spinach
4. Oranges
5. Garlic
6. Apples
7. Soybeans
8. Carrots
9. Hot red peppers
10. Green tea

Lycopene This gives **tomatoes, watermelons** and **pink grapefruit** their color. A powerful antioxidant, it protects against heart disease and certain cancers, particularly prostate cancer.

There is a dark side to phytochemicals, though. For example, *coumarin*, a blood-thinning agent found in sweet clovers and woodruff, is poisonous to livestock and is the principal ingredient of the rat killer, *Warfarin*. It is also the most frequently used oral anticoagulant medicine.

Heritage Seeds

There's much talk these days of heritage seeds, which refer to old, non-hybrid varieties of vegetables, many of them consigned to history. Sadly, more than 80 per cent of the seed varieties sold a century ago are not available today. Seed catalogues offer mostly what are called modern *F1 hybrids* (or first filial generation, from a cross between two strains). These were developed in tandem with the rise of agribusiness and multinational companies, as commercial growers and retailers demanded easy-to-grow, uniform produce that would give high yields, could be picked early, would withstand shipping and have a long shelf life. The problem with these hybrids is that they do not come true from seed (i.e., the seeds do not produce the same plant but are highly variable) so gardeners can't save their seed, but have to buy fresh every year (sold by, who else, but the multinational companies).

With growers planting only one or two varieties of a vegetable, it means acres of what is essentially a monoculture—the antithesis of biodiversity, the agricultural drug addict, the killer of soil richness (for more on the benefits of biodiversity, see Chapter 5). Further, in a monoculture, a small disease or pest infestation can rapidly reach plague proportions and wipe out the entire lot. Greater species diversity means fewer plants are affected and there's a substantially smaller toll.

The other vital element is genetic diversity. These heritage varieties contain a treasure trove of genetic material which could be of critical importance down the road. It is known that species suffering genetic impoverishment eventually weaken and die out. The bigger the genetic pool, the stronger and more adaptable the "swimmers." As Pauline Lloyd, editor of the *Vegan News*, points out, "No one can predict with any great certainty exactly which genetic characteristics will be of importance in 50 or more years time. Nor can anyone know which pests and diseases will be around then or what the climate will be like. It is, therefore, vitally important that we maintain genetic diversity by preserving as many different species of plants as possible."[4]

Internationally, a number of seed banks are storing life for an uncertain future. At Kew Gardens in England, they aim to treat and store seeds of more than 25,000 species of plants and expect them to remain viable for between 200 and 1,000 years. In addition, various seed exchanges and small suppliers specialize in heritage seeds. Seeds of Diversity Canada, for instance, boasts that its members currently grow 675 varieties of tomatoes, 275 varieties of beans, 76 varieties of peppers, 45 varieties of potatoes, 37 varieties of squash, 37 varieties of peas and 21 varieties of garlic. Seeds of Change offers a huge range of organic vegetables, herbs, cover crops and flowers (see Resources).

Heritage (or heirloom) varieties are better for us and the earth. They do not require artificial fertilizers, are less susceptible to diseases and pests, and so spare us chemical pollution. They usually taste better and keep just as well as commercially grown varieties, and they produce over a period of time instead of all at once.

It's just a step from decoding genetic diversity to genetic modification or engineering, a process in which genetic material from one plant, or bacteria, is inserted into another. Usually applied to crop plants such as corn, potatoes and beets, it is done to give them herbicide, insect or virus resistance. In the first case, it is supposed to allow the spraying of weeds without killing the crop. In the other cases, it is supposed to reduce the amount of pesticide applied. However, critics of these so-called *Frankenplants* claim they don't lessen the chemical assault and do run other risks such as harming beneficial insects, making pests more resistant, pollinating with wild species and escaping as mutant monsters. Another problem is that there is no requirement that genetically engineered (GE) plants, seeds and foodstuffs containing them be labeled as such.

Heritage seeds, such as these blue beans, preserve genetic diversity as well as rich taste and color.

By permission of Adrian Raeside

North American agribusiness has been quick to embrace such GE plants as corn, cotton, soybeans, potatoes and canola. In 1999, more than 70 million acres of transgenic crops were planted in the United States alone. A decade-long study by British scientists released in February, 2001, found no evidence that four GE crops (beets, corn, canola and potatoes) could spread in the wild and become "super-weeds."[5] But that addresses only one environmental risk.

The real green revolution would be to adjust our crops and agricultural practices to the nature of nature, instead of trying fruitlessly to make nature adjust to the demands of monoculture. For me, bioengineering is a long way from Aldo Leopold's notion of "intelligent tinkering." We may tinker to our regret. Change will be cumbersome and slow in large-scale agriculture, which makes it even more vital for the home gardener to grow heritage and non-GE seeds, creating a richly diverse, healthy garden that tastes as good as it looks.

And So to Bed

The first decision about growing edibles is where to put them. Most need lots of sun and fertile soil. Since the Victorian decree of "a place for everything and everything in its place," vegetables have been ghettoized, rather than mingled with other plants. There are pros and cons to both approaches. The exclusive veggie bed is easier to access, tend and harvest; many vegetables benefit from being grown together; and the ground can be cleared and amended without disturbing permanent plantings. Mingling them allows more scope for their ornamental qualities (multi-colored lettuces make marvelous edging, and scarlet runner beans will scramble colorfully over an arbor in no time); breaks the "monoculture mode"; permits integration of

perennial vegetables such as asparagus and rhubarb; and profits from the beneficial insects attracted by flowers.

Since vegetables require rich, well-prepared soil, they are often grown in raised beds. These should be no wider than five feet (1.5 m) so you can reach in from both sides and can be of any height. Depending on how good your soil and drainage, the beds can be just gently mounded earth, or slightly raised with a board edging, or made higher with permanent, constructed walls of brick or stone (the best solution if you have heavy clay). Higher raised beds are real back-savers and easy to tend even from a wheelchair (see Chapter 12 for more on accessible gardening). Raised beds warm up quickly in spring and can be intensively planted, making the most of a small area.

Raised beds can be simply mounded earth, as in this bed of lettuce. The flowers planted nearby draw a host of beneficial insects.

Pressure-Treated Wood

How safe is it to use pressure-treated wood for raised vegetable beds? This green-tinted wood has had a chemical called *chromated copper arsenate* (CCA) forced into its fibers in a pressure chamber. CCA is made up of copper and arsenic, which are toxic to the bacteria, fungi and bugs that might attack the wood, and

Alternatives to Pressure-Treated Wood

- ACQ© pressure-treated wood. ACQ is alkaline copper quat, a mix of copper and a quaternary ammonium compound, which is not considered hazardous, uses recycled copper, and is supposed to last as long as CCA-treated lumber. It may not be easy to find, however.
- Manufactured lumber that combines waste wood fiber with recycled plastic (*Trex* for example), or all-plastic wood (*Superwood*); they can be worked like wood, are non-toxic, resist pests and never need painting.
- Woods that naturally resist decay, such as Western red cedar, Douglas fir and redwood.
- Wood protected with a non-toxic, environmentally friendly preservative such as *Lifetime Wood Treatment*, which needs only one application.

chromium, which acts as a binding agent. These are noxious chemicals and anyone working with pressure-treated wood should wear gloves, eye and skin protection and a dust mask. Don't put the sawdust in your compost and definitely avoid burning this wood.

The question is can the chemicals leach into the soil and affect the veggies growing there? Three major studies of vegetables grown in arsenic-enhanced soil have shown the amount of arsenic absorbed by the plants is actually quite insignificant—carrots grown in soil with 24 ppm total arsenic had an arsenic level of 0.11 ppm, while carrots grown in soil with no added arsenic contained 0.05 ppm.[6] The danger comes more from the exposed wood surfaces since the arsenic migrates to the surface and any leaching, no matter how small, means you or your children can pick it up just by touching the wood. Painting it with a water-repellent stain or paint will help, and you can use a heavy plastic liner inside the raised bed, but why bother?

Digging

A lot of books advise you to double dig new beds, which involves taking soil out two spits deep (a spit equals the depth of the business part of a shovel), the top spit being topsoil and the lower one being subsoil. The topsoil is relieved of weeds, compost is incorporated into the subsoil and it's all put back, keeping the topsoil on top. Single digging is the same to just one spade depth.

This backbreaking labor (get a case of beer and find a couple of strong and willing helpers) is worth doing if your soil is really compacted and undernourished. It will allow air and water to penetrate, and the organic matter you add will get all the little soil critters going. Vegetables will reflect the quality of your site preparation in their yield, size and quality, so it's not worth stinting. The good news is you should only have to do it once. Subsequently, if you mulch and compost well, the worms will do the work. Just keep on top of the weeds and don't walk on the beds (or you'll shatter that fluffy, airy soil structure).

Tilling

It may seem easy to bash around with a rototiller, and certainly rototilling is widely considered standard procedure. But, in a word, *don't*. Every time you turn the soil, you bring to the surface weed seeds that have been lurking deep in the soil just waiting for the chance to germinate. And don't think they aren't there. One pigweed plant (*Amaranth*) can produce 117,000 seeds in a single year. As many as 1,140 seeds per square foot (.09 m^2) can survive in the top inch (2.5 cm) of soil alone, and can remain viable for years. In 1879, botanist William Beal buried a bottle containing 1,000 seeds of 20 common weeds. Unearthed in 1980, the 101-year-old seeds still produced 26 enthusiastic seedlings.[7]

Tilling the soil also reduces the size of the soil particles, which then dry out and may be lost to erosion by wind and water. (Just $\frac{3}{64}$ of an inch/1 mm loss per acre adds up to 4.5 tons/4.08 metric tons!) As you walk behind the machine, you compact the soil as quickly as you turn it up. Tilling also shatters the soil horizons, wreaks havoc on the earthworm population (no, they do not "grow back" if they are cut into pieces) and causes catastrophic upheaval to the vast, underground micro-metropolis (see Chapter 2 for more on the underground population). Take the no-till approach, which has been called *synergistic agriculture* and relies solely on the alchemy of healthy soil, mulch and benign human neglect.

Crop Rotation

Why rotate crops? Basically, to reduce pests and diseases, though it originated with high-nitrogen fertilizing when crops requiring a lot of nitrogen were planted first, followed by crops requiring less. But organic gardening keeps nitrogen levels consistent, so that doesn't apply. Still, rotation is advisable since crops grown in the same place for two or more years draw pests and disease which colonize the soil waiting for their next banquet, and some plants accumulate toxic allelopathic compounds (see "Allelopathy," Chapter 4).

There are six major vegetable groups:

- Brassicas (Brassicaceae family) including cauliflower, broccoli, kale and cabbage; susceptible to clubroot
- Onions/garlic (Alliaceae family); susceptible to white rot
- Potatoes/tomatoes/eggplant (Solanaceae family); susceptible to nematodes

- Carrot/celery (Apiaceae family)
- Legumes including beans/peas (Fabaceae family)
- Marrows (Cucurbitaceae family) including squash, cucumber, melon and pumpkin

You should rotate at least the first three, and ideally all six. This can get complicated, but if you avoid replanting any crop in the same place for at least three years, you should be fine. Check the veggie families—if you don't know that potatoes and tomatoes are in the same family, you might plant them in succession and wonder why they succumb. Always include legumes since their roots have nodules containing "nitrogen-fixing" bacteria that capture nitrogen from the air and make it available to plants. And remember the more organic matter, the larger and more diverse the population of disease-suppressing organisms.

Companion Planting

This organic garden combines different vegetable crops with herbs and flowers; a white row cover protects tender seedlings from flies which would lay their eggs on them.

There is a whole complex web of connections between plants (both positive and negative), involving all kinds of root exudates, microorganisms, biochemicals and insects (see "Allelopathy," Chapter 4). Exploiting these can turn every gardener into a Dolly Levi, matching those that like and keeping apart those that don't. For

Love/Hate Relationships

Vegetables	Perfect Matches	Mismatches
Beans	Brassicas, carrot	Fennel, onion
Beets	Brassicas esp. kohlrabi, bush beans, onion	Pole beans
Brassicas	Pea, potato, garlic, cucumber, bush beans	Pole beans, strawberry
Carrot	Leek, lettuce, pea, onion, garlic, tomato	Dill
Cucumber	Legumes, radish	Potato, aromatic herbs especially sage
Lettuce	Carrot, radish, cucumber, strawberry	
Corn	Pole beans, potato, cucumber	Tomatoes
Onion	Lettuce, tomato, leek	Legumes
Peas	Beans, carrot, cucumber, potato, corn	Onion, garlic
Potato	Legumes, brassicas, corn	Cucumber, tomato, cherries
Sweet pepper	Eggplant	Brassicas
Tomato	Asparagus, carrot, onion, garlic, radish	Potato, fennel, kohlrabi, corn

Not just pretty faces, sunflowers are a valuable addition to the vegetable garden, as they emit chemicals that discourage weeds.

instance, tomatoes protect asparagus against the asparagus beetle but render potatoes more susceptible to potato blight. Carrot roots produce a substance beneficial to peas, while onions and leeks help repel the carrot fly.

Follow the lead of native Americans by growing the "three sisters"—pole beans, corn and squash—together. A perfect example of sibling harmony, the

Shaping Up

Traditional garden beds are rectangular or round, but they can be any shape you want to make them. This S shape, or keyhole garden, as gardener/illustrator Diane Rhoades calls it, was devised by Australia's aborigines who made companion planting an art form. The shape not only discourages insects, it provides a huge amount of edges, where plants thrive (see "On the Edge," Chapter 5), and easy access via the "keyholes." And it's beautiful. (The garden in this illustration is 22 feet/6.7m long and 12 feet/3.6m across.)

Illustration by:
Diane Rhoades, Garden Crafts for Kids, 50 Great Reasons to Get Your Hands Dirty, *New York: Sterling/Lark, 1995.*

corn supports the beans, the beans supply nitrogen in the soil, while the ground-covering squash keeps out weeds and conserves moisture. Traditionally planted in a circular shape (the "circle of life"), this companionable planting makes the most of the space, and, whether the native Americans realized it or not, improves the corn's sex life. Corn should always be planted in a block, never in a straight row, for good pollination.

Other ideal companions are plants that either attract beneficial insects or "trap" or repel insects that might otherwise head for your edibles. Common ones are nasturtiums (*Tropaeolum majus*), which trap aphids and attract hover flies; candytuft (*Iberis*), which deters flea beetles. Also effective are the aromatic herbs, including sage (*Salvia*) and rosemary (*Rosmarinus*), which repel cabbage moths and carrot flies, rue (*Ruta graveolens*), which deters Japanese beetles, tansy (*Tanacetum*), which protects against striped cucumber beetles and squash bugs, and thyme (*Thymus*), which discourages cabbage worms (see Chapter 9 for more on herbal companions).

For further pest control: Pick bugs and eggs off by hand, or hose them off with a strong stream of water. Attract birds and provide habitats for toads, ground beetles and other greedy pest destroyers (for more ideas, see Chapter 7).

The edible garden affords a close-up look at some of nature's most intimate workings and a clear (sometimes all-too-clear) demonstration of natural cause and effect. It is challenging, rewarding and always instructive. The lessons learned in the vegetable patch can be readily applied to the rest of your garden, your community and the earth—and "store-bought" will never taste the same again.

Marigold Misconception

Marigolds are often hailed for their ability to rid the earth of nasty nematodes. They do, but to get them to do it, you have to plant the entire bed in marigolds and grow them for a whole season. Dotting them about your veggie garden will have little impact on nematodes—though they will still draw beneficial insects and possibly confuse pests with their scent.

9

Please Step on the Thyme

He who would know humility
Must weed a bed of thyme.

ADELMA GRENIER SIMMONS, 1964

Ever since an ancient Chaldean wrote a paean to frankincense, an Egyptian embalmer perfumed his oil with chamomile and a Roman chef shaped a rosemary topiary, herbs have left a scented trail through human history. It's a rare gardener who wouldn't have herbs, even if it's just a pot of parsley or a couple of basil plants. We tend to think of herbs as the small or bushy aromatic plants so vital in the kitchen but in fact "herb" is a large umbrella covering trees, shrubs, vines, ferns, mosses and fungi as well as perennials, annuals and biennials—indeed, all plants valued for their culinary, medicinal, cosmetic, industrial, pesticidal or colorant properties.

With their texture, color, healing and fragrance, herbs are a sensual ingredient of any garden, and enliven any dish with their fresh flavors. They often add a shot of vitamins and minerals to boot, and can be better aids to digestion than a carton of Tums. Garlic, for instance, which keeps bugs off your roses, also preys on any gastric "bugs" you may pick up on your travels, preventing diarrhea and vomiting. Astringent herbs stimulate the liver and gall bladder, making fats easier to digest, while peppermint soothes the digestive tract and freshens the breath (hence the ubiquitous after-dinner mints).

Tisane, anyone? Few things in the garden are as sensually satisfying as a basket of fresh, aromatic and tasty herbs.

The pungent spices such as chili, ginger and pepper so common in the cuisine of hot countries give your metabolism a kick and make you sweat—the body's form of air-conditioning. The ancient Greeks knew that chewing parsley would sweeten onion or garlic breath, while caraway, fennel and dill contain oils that relieve flatulence (to everyone else's relief).

Aromatic Herbs

In the days of poor sanitation and even poorer personal hygiene, aromatic herbs known as "strewing herbs" were scattered about the floor to mask room odors and keep flies away— tansy (*Tanacetum*), sweet woodruff (*Galium*

Favorite Culinary Herbs

Basil (*Ocimum basilicum*)
What would tomatoes be without sun-spiced basil? Available in several forms from large-leafed green to frilly purple and small-leaved bush types. It's a real heat-lover and shrinks from the slightest chill. Pinch back to prevent legginess and nip off any flowers.

Coriander (*Coriandrum sativum*)
The seeds are coriander; the leaves are cilantro. You either love or hate the smell (some call it piquant; I think it smells like ancient gym socks). It's hard to believe, but in *Thousand and One Nights*, it was employed as an aphrodisiac. One of the oldest spices, it was used by the ancient Romans to preserve meat; now, modern cooks seeking authentic Chinese and Latin American tastes toss handfuls of cilantro on everything. It's also an *aide digestif* and flatulence-reliever.

Dill (*Anethum graveolens*)
A witching herb, it was used both to cast spells and protect against them. Its name comes from the Old Norse *dilla*, meaning to lull, referring to its ability to soothe. Apparently, it cures hiccups, among other things. Feathery foliage is wonderfully aromatic and its umbels of small yellow flowers are used to flavor dill pickles.

Parsley (*Petroselinum crispum*)
Don't leave that garnish on your plate—it's full of vitamins and minerals, improves digestion and is a diuretic. Curly or flat (otherwise called Italian), parsley is easy to grow as an edging plant or in pots. It likes moist rich soil and I think tastes best after a day of rain.

Sage (*Salvia officinalis*)
A herb with a history, the culinary sages are among the most ornamental. Their distinctive leaves resembling pebbly suede come in gray-green, silver-green, gold, purple and various combinations thereof. Sage fits in any flower border or looks splendid anchoring a terracotta pot. Bees and hummingbirds will come to the flowers. Older plants develop a woody structure and rebound in spring when cut back.

Rosemary (*Rosmarinus officinalis*)
A must-have herb that is reputed to restore memory, ward off witches and cure hangovers. Well, it stimulates the circulation and relieves muscle tension at least. Its scent and flavor is indispensable in the kitchen. Though grown mostly as an annual, it can be wintered over inside in a cool, bright spot.

Thyme (*Thymus* spp.)
Small-leaved shrubs or prostrate spreaders, they have a range of foliage, flowers and scents, including lemon, lime, orange, mint, caraway and nutmeg. Honey bees adore the flowers. Not only a pot herb, it is a prime ingredient in cough remedies and mouthwashes.

Mint (*Mentha* spp.)
Given the chance, mint would take over the world, so it definitely must be confined to a pot. It also comes in a dazzling olfactory array—apple, banana, chocolate, ginger, orange, pineapple and good old English-mint-sauce mint (*M. spicata*).

With leaves like pebbly suede, sage (Salvia) is as ornamental as it is flavorful.

Once believed to cure 43 ills of the flesh and spirit, lavender has an evocative scent that relieves stress and restores balance.

odoratum), mint (*Mentha*) and chamomile (*Chamaemelum*) were popular. People wore fragrant flowers or oils to cover body odor or sometimes to ward off infection: sixteenth-century Europeans carried pouches of rosemary (*Rosmarinus*) as a defense against the plague. Actually, they weren't far wrong. The essential oils of many herbs are powerful antiseptics. Cinnamon oil reportedly kills typhoid germs in 12 minutes, while thyme (*Thymus*) oil has 12 times the germ-killing strength of carbolic acid.[1] (The essential oils of many fragrant plants are used in aromatherapy, but given their potency, never apply them directly to the skin.)

Probably the most popular scented herb is lavender (*Lavandula*), which perfumed the sheets, soaps and pomades of ancient Greeks and Romans. In medieval times, it was also a strewing herb and "a medicine believed to cure 43 ills of the flesh and spirit."[2] At one time, it was a very popular culinary herb, but our taste for that has changed (though Tessa Evelegh offers a mean recipe for lavender cookies in her book, *Lavender*).

Today, lavender is a mainstay of the perfume industry and, along with roses and lilacs, is one of the most evocative scents, in western culture at least. No garden should be without its purple flower spires, gray-green foliage and scent that helps relieve stress and restore balance. Bees love it and it produces ambrosial honey. Though not perennial in much of Canada and the northern states, it's worth growing as an annual along a pathway or in a pot. Originally a Mediterranean plant, it appreciates good drainage, alkaline soil and lots of sun. Mind, when I was in England one July, it was cold and damp to the point of rawness, and the lavender was magnificent—great undulations of purple set off against deep boxwoods and brick paths the color of centuries.

Great Pretenders

My garden would never be without what I call "the great pretenders"—plants that smell like something completely different. You expect mint to smell like mint, but what an unexpected delight to rub the irresistibly downy leaves of the geranium, *Pelargonium tomentosum*, and inhale a minty scent that is practically edible.

Scented geraniums (*Pelargonium* spp.) are downright addictive. Every year, I discover more—apple, apricot, lime, orange and coconut, nutmeg, pine, rose, strawberry and the famous lemon. Their foliage is as diverse as their scents, from lemon's crisply lobed green leaves to peppermint's fuzzy silver scallops, from skeleton rose's filigree to nutmeg's small frilly discs that any elf would call suede.

They do flower, but the blooms are nothing like the whacking great blobs of the common annual geraniums. They're smaller, more open and usually pink, though some like *P.* 'Mrs. Taylor' and *P.* 'Clorinda' are flashier, if that's where your taste runs.

They thrive in sun in pots, window boxes and baskets, but are equally happy in the ground as long as their feet aren't too wet. Cuttings root practically overnight so you'll have plenty to give away, or use as flavorings and in potpourri.

Equally great pretenders are some of the sages, especially pineapple sage (*Salvia elegans* or *rutilans*), which not only has leaves that out-pineapple pineapple but also glorious red

How Sweet It Is

Indulge your sweet tooth, or just your herbal curiosity, and grow some stevia (*Stevia rebaudiana*). This South American native belonging to the daisy family is a natural sweetener—in fact, its leaves are packed with compounds up to 300 times sweeter than sugar, without the calories. Grown as an annual in Canada and northern states, it has a bushy form (with diligent pinching-back) and can reach three feet (91 cm) in height. It likes sandy soil and excellent drainage. Nipping off the little white flowers keeps the leaves their sweetest. (One caution: stevia's pollen is highly allergenic, so allergy-sufferers will have to stick to sugar.) Pick the leaves and let them dry in the sun for 24 hours. Store them in an airtight jar and grind them before using.

flowers that have hummingbirds swooning with delight. There's also a sage with a tropical bent—the mixed-fruit-scented *S. dorisiana*—and a tangerine sage (a cultivar of *S. elegans*), but pineapple tops my list.

You could put together a whole "pucker-up" garden with lemon pretenders. There's lemon: balm (*Melissa officinalis*), basil (*Ocimum americanum* and *O. basilicum*), bergamot (*Monarda citriodora*), catnip (*Nepeta cataria* ssp. *citriodora*), eucalyptus (*Eucalyptus citriodora*), geraniums (*Pelargonium citronellum*, *P.* 'Citrosa' and *P. crispum*), grass (*Cymbopogon citratus*), marigold (*Tagetes tenuifolia*), thyme (*Thymus* x *citriodorus* and *T. pulegioides*) and verbena (*Aloysia triphylla*). Some of them are a tad too "Pledge furniture polish" for me and some may be too vigorous for a small space, but all that lemon would certainly be refreshing. Lemon-scented geraniums (*P.* 'Citrosa') are supposed to keep mosquitoes away, but my husband, whom they find delectable, remains unconvinced.

Hip Hips

A rich source of vitamin C (as well as vitamin A, B, E, K and niacin), rose hips can be boiled for a tonic/tea and taken for colds and flu, or used like cranberries in jams or sauce. Such a conserve was used in the Middle Ages as a cough remedy. Use the biggest, ripest hips from roses that have not been sprayed with anything toxic (*Rosa rugosa* produces excellent ones). Be sure to boil them for at least 10 or 15 minutes until they split, and then strain off the tea.

When cooking with them, cut them in half and scoop out the seeds before proceeding. Or boil them and press them through a sieve to make a rose hip purée. They can also be dried and stored in tightly sealed jars.

Healing Herbs

Herbs' most colorful history is in their medicinal uses, which go back to the ancients. Herbal remedies were, after all, the foundation of modern medicine, and many of today's drugs are plant-derived, for example, the heart drug, digoxin, comes from foxgloves (*Digitalis*); the heart stimulant, atropine, from deadly nightshade (*Atropa belladonna*); and the painkiller, codeine, from the opium poppy (*Papaver somniferum*). More recently, taxol from the Pacific yew (*Taxus brevifolia*) is showing promise in cancer treatment. In sixth-century Europe, the

---

Rose Hip Jam

2 lbs (900 g) rose hips

4 green apples

2 1/2 lbs (1.1 kg) white sugar

1/3 cup (80 mL) lemon juice

Boil the rose hips in 2 pints (1 L) of water and cook until tender. Rub through a fine sieve to separate seeds and make a purée. Peel and core the apples, then cook them separately in a small amount of water until soft. Rub the apples through a sieve. Combine the rose hip and apple purées with the sugar and lemon juice. Bring to full boil, then boil for an additional 15 minutes. Place in small sterilized jelly jars and seal.[3]

monastery "physic garden" was the pharmacy of the day (and precursor to our botanical gardens). Aboriginal peoples on all continents amassed a vast knowledge of plants' medicinal powers, and there are few drugs in use today that they weren't aware of first.

Although I am no herbalist, I revel in herbs for their sensual attributes. There is a wealth of books and web sites devoted to herbal healing that you can consult. One caveat, actually two: many herbal remedies are not recommended for pregnant women, and everyone should exercise caution in self-medicating with herbal remedies. They may react with other prescription drugs or with each other. Herbalists say these remedies are superior because they contain the plant's whole chemical makeup so there is a synergistic or holistic effect, i.e., the active ingredient(s) work better in combination with the other elements. In contrast, most drugs are synthetic versions of the isolated active ingredient. I believe the guiding principle is that herbs can heal, rather than cure.

But the role of herbs in medicine, as well as myth and folklore, is endlessly fascinating. Who can't be intrigued by the sixteenth-century Doctrine of Signatures—the belief that a plant could treat whatever part of the body it resembled? For

University of British Columbia's Physick Garden: doctors in sixth-century Europe drew on the pharmacies of the day, the herb-filled physic gardens in the monasteries.

instance, lungwort (*Pulmonaria*) with its spotted leaves was thought to look like the lung, so was used to treat respiratory ailments, while the red sap of bloodroot (*Sanguinaria canadensis*) was a cure for bad blood. Then there was the mystical mandrake (*Mandragora officinarum*), whose roots contain the powerful relaxant, hyoscine. The only problem was the medieval folk believed, that since the root resembled a human figure, anyone trying to dig it up would join the root in its screaming death throes. The solution was to tie a dog to the plant and have the animal drag it out of the ground, while they plugged their ears![4]

Dr. Edward Bach, an English homeopath in the 1920s, devised what he called flower remedies, which were tinctures made from 38 wild plants, including rock rose (*Cistus*), to treat "terror," scleranthus (*Scleranthus*) for "indecision without resort to advice" and white chestnut (*Aesculus hippocastanum*) for "unwanted thoughts and mental arguments." They are still available, by the way. Check out www.bachcentre.com.

Caraway (*Carum carvi*) seeds were once given to lovers as a guard against fickleness and fed to pigeons to keep them from straying. Costmary (*Chrysanthemum balsamita*) was also called *Bible leaf* because it was used as a prayer book marker (and nibbled on during protracted sermons to keep the listener awake).[5] Who knew?

Medical uses also explain why so many plants have body parts or specific maladies in their common names: boneset, spleenwort, goutweed, rupturewort, liverwort, skullcap, feverfew. In Latin, *officinalis* means "of the pharmacopoeia," so any plant with that term in its name was used for healing.

Herbs aren't just taken in tonics and tinctures: there's a worldwide history of burning them as incense to purify, bless, soothe or sanctify. For instance, smoldering bundles of rosemary, lavender and pine added a distinctive odor of sanctity to sacred rites in the goddess cultures of the Mediterranean.[6] Today, we content ourselves with diffusers that release the heady fragrances of essential oils into the air.

Herbs in the Garden

Just like vegetables, you can plant herbs together in a dedicated area—a raised bed brings them to easy sniffing and harvesting level—or scatter them hither and thither. Scattering them allows you to take advantage of their potent insect repellent or attractant properties. For instance, lemon balm (*Melissa officinalis*) wards off squash bugs; basil (*Ocimum basilicum*) repels thrips, flies and mosquitoes; and chervil (*Anthriscus cerefolium*) keeps aphids from munching your lettuce. Borage (*Borago officinalis*) makes a great ally for tomatoes, squash and strawberries, deterring those monstrous tomato hornworms and drawing bees like flies. In fact, it's so neighborly it helps any plant it's near fight off pests and disease. Dill (*Anethum graveolens*) attracts hover flies and predatory wasps, while larkspur (*Consolida*) attracts Japanese beetles.

Most herbs love sandy, gravelly soil, so they will gravitate to pathways where they often grow better than in the bed where they were first planted. I put woolly thyme (*Thymus pseudolanuginosus*) along a path, hoping it would spread and sort of puddle about— which it promptly did. Our garden was a site on a garden tour that year, so there I was awaiting the release of fragrance at every step, only to watch each visitor come down the path, pause and carefully step *over* the thyme. I finally put up a sign that read: *Please Step on the Thyme.*

A raised bed, such as this one overflowing with variegated and silvery-green sages in North Vancouver's Park & Tilford Gardens, brings herbs to easy sniffing and harvesting level.

Dill's lacy texture and chartreuse flowers easily rival the flamboyant charms of satiny magenta poppies.

The traditional form of herb garden is a knot garden, which is a geometric shape divided into a symmetrical pattern of sections. Each section is then planted with a specific herb or family of herbs. The center is customarily anchored by a sundial or large pot, and the sections are neatly rimmed with low hedges of boxwood (*Buxus*), lavender (*Lavandula*) or lavender cotton (*Santolina*). A knot garden can be open, meaning it has pathways between the sections, or closed, i.e., solidly planted. Elaborate geometric patterns make the hedges look as though they intertwine—hence the name. All very divine. All very labor-intensive. Do this only if you have no other gardening interests and can derive complete and utter satisfaction from constantly snipping back wayward boxwood, lavender or santolina.

Another option is an intriguing spiral design, thought up by Bill Mollison, the guru of permaculture. It involves building up a spiral shape like an upright pointed seashell. The herbs are then planted in the gradually ascending bed. Drought-lovers go at the top, while those needing more water occupy the lower levels. This design also packs a lot of plants in the space. And the spiral is such an organically beautiful form, symbolizing growth, evolution and the continuity of life—perfect for the healing garden.

Pot Herbs

The easiest way to create an herb garden is to plant them in containers. Make sure the pots are large enough and have excellent drainage. Be creative—you can come up with some stunning combinations. Surround a tall bushy herb, such as rosemary (*Rosmarinus officinalis*), with lower-growing ones like marjoram (*Origanum*), thyme (*Thymus* spp.), or parsley (*Petroselinum crispum*). Purple and green basils (*Ocimum basilicum*) are fantastic paired with orange pot marigolds (*Calendula*). Do a whole pot of mixed sages (*Salvia officinalis*), and get extra containers for all the scented geraniums (*Pelargonium* spp.) you will be unable to resist. The exceptions to containerdom are dill (*Anethum graveolens*) and fennel (*Foeniculum*), which I find do better in the ground. Statuesque but delicate, they act like a lacy scrim. Dill's chartreuse umbels sashaying among satiny magenta poppies (*Papaver*) is something to behold.

To catch sight of white Japanese anemones bobbing and weaving through the fronds of bronze fennel is to realize that herbs are bewitching additions to the healing garden, even if you never whip up a pesto, brew a tea or prepare a tincture. Few plants cast such a spell or give so much—in terms of sensory delight, facts and lore, mood enhancement, and healing—as do herbs.

A Garden
for the Senses

*I rubbed rose petals on my cheeks,
nibbled mint leaves, crushed lemon balm
all over my half-bald head, and I admit,
actually kissed the fluffy pink peonies
that I had transplanted years ago from
my mother's garden after she died.
Breathing in peony perfume, you
participate in the immortal.*

TORONTO WRITER MICHELE LANDSBERG
DISCOVERS THE GARDEN'S SENSUAL
HEALING POWERS WHILE BEING TREATED
FOR BREAST CANCER.[1]

To surrender to the sensory garden's enticements is to blissfully satisfy the body, mind and spirit. But how exactly we perceive and process the thousands of sights, sounds, smells, touches and tastes we encounter every day still defies complete explanation. Scientists, philosophers and psychologists have all had a go, but admit that, ultimately, our perceptions are totally subjective.

It *is* agreed that sensory stimulation is vital to healthy brain function and actually gives the little-gray-cell connections a beneficial workout. Conversely, "sudden and nearly complete deprivation of stimulation through the five senses can lead to dramatic changes in the brain's efficiency with a partial loss of memory, a lowering of the I.Q., personality changes including withdrawal, hallucinations, and even an abnormal electroencephalogram."[2] By contrast, in over-stimulating situations when everything's going crazy and we cry that we just can't think straight, when there's too much information for the brain to process, it starts coming up with irrelevant responses.

Stressed-out or whacked-out, there is renewal and healing in the garden's timeless green rhythms and deeper harmonies that touch all our senses. The skin feels not just touch but heat and cold, and pain; our bodies experience hunger and thirst; and a sense of balance is not simply a matter of remaining upright. There's also what biologist Martin Galloway calls our sixth sense: intellectual stimulation. In the peering and poking, the sowing and tending, the garden is a perpetual journey of discovery.

Sight

We revel in the garden's wanton displays of color, but color "…is a paradox. It exists only in light, which to the human eye seems almost colorless."[3] The hues we see depend on how an object absorbs, transmits or reflects the different wavelengths of light. Light sensors in our eyes called *rods* and *cones* convert the light energy into electrical impulses which zip along nerve fibers to the optic nerve which, in turn, sends messages to the visual cortex in the brain. But the eye is not a camera; the process is like a computer "designed to construct a representation of reality."[4] The real virtual reality.

Our lives have been permeated with color since a caveman chose red pigment to paint with. And just as one person's gray is another's violet, there are unique cultural perceptions—for instance, North Americans regard red/orange/yellow as hot and exciting, blue/green as cool and calming, while the Japanese regard blue/green as good and red/purple as bad. Here, the color of mourning is traditionally black; elsewhere, it may be white, purple or gold.

Our physical and emotional reactions to colors are tinted by our moods, our state of health and time of life as well as by the baggage of associations we all carry. Perceptions change with every turn of the kaleidoscope. Scarlet by itself may be overpowering but thrilling when balanced by its complementary color, green. Add some varying tones (a deeper burgundy, a bright chartreuse, for example) and things really start happening.

Working from nature's boundless palette, the garden is an ever-changing painting, brushed by light.

Red A primary color of passion, red makes the heart beat faster. It also stimulates the appetite, boosts blood pressure and makes your breath come quicker. For the Cherokee people, red symbolized success, and the red spirit oversaw long life and recovery from illness. It seems that men generally prefer orange-red tones while women like blue-reds. Children (and hummingbirds) love them all.

Orange Named for the citrus fruit, the word came to denote fruitfulness. With its connotation of flames and fire, it also summons feelings of warmth and power. Although stimulating, it is thought to lessen hostility and irritability, and engender optimism. Butterflies love orange flowers.

Yellow Most easily seen from a distance and by the visually impaired, primary yellow captures the sun and embodies cheerfulness, playfulness and creativity. It also stimulates clear thinking. Golden yellow represents faith, constancy, wisdom and glory. Negative connotations include cowardice, aging and illness.

Blue The third primary color, it's the color of the sky, the sea and serenity, of faith, peace and loyalty. Dark blue is formal and respectful, while light blue is clean, refreshing and

These hardy geraniums and purple sage combine the restfulness of pink with the regal tones of purple, the color of wealth and power.

A garlic chive artlessly creates a sublime curvilinear sculpture. Green is nature's primary color, underlying many of the garden's healing aspects.

cool. Few flowers are really a true blue, but azure butterfly delphiniums (*Delphinium grandiflorum*) come close. Once, I showed some to Ruth, a dear lady with Alzheimer's. "Oh," she said joyfully, "It's delicious...I could lick it!"

Pink One of the most popular colors in the garden, perhaps because it is so restful. (Studies have shown that violent prisoners calmed down when put in pink cells, at least in the short term. In the long term, they became *more* violent, so as in everything, moderation is a good thing.)

Purple A regal color whose name comes from the Greek *porphura* referring to a sort of shellfish from which the dye called *Tyrian purple* was derived. The dye was so expensive to produce that only VIPs got to use it; aptly, this rich color denotes wealth, leadership and power. And it's attractive to butterflies.

Black Often associated with evil and mourning, black also conjures mystery, depression and strength. The fascination with black flowers hasn't abated since Alexandre Dumas wrote *The Black Tulip* in 1850. Most of them aren't really black; they only seem so because we see them in relationship to other colors.

White The color of purity, truth, cleanliness and a northern winter, it projects calmness and inner peace. It is the choice for the gardens of evening when it seems to capture and hold twilight's last gleaming. Many white flowers release their strongest scent at night to lure pollinating moths.

Green Nature's primary color, green represents renewal and freshness, health and growth, fertility and abundance. The predominance of green underlies many of the garden's healing qualities, from lowering blood pressure, relieving pain and reducing stress to promoting positive feelings, increasing alpha waves in the brain and creating a sense of harmony and well-being.

Of course, nature's colors are not provided for our benefit; flowers are really just out there looking for sex. And their obliging pollinators often see them quite differently. For instance, honeybees are finely tuned to ultra-violet light and they see patterns on flowers that are invisible to our eyes, patterns that are essentially guides to the sweet reward of nectar. Whatever colors you pick to soothe or revive your spirits, they will be appreciated even more by their humming, buzzing, fluttering suitors.

Visual appeal isn't limited to color. The free-form and geometric shapes nature is so fond of drawing combine in a never-ending gallery of still lifes and "motion pictures." They in turn are filled with a seemingly inexhaustible supply of textures and patterns, from the artichoke's (*Cynara*) shocking fuzzy flower clasped by fleshy green fingers, to the canna's (*Canna*) smoothly striped umbrella of a leaf, from the dwarf spirea's (*Spiraea*) cushion-tidy mound to the blue spruce's (*Picea pungens* 'Glauca') towering triangle.

Scent

Fragrance is the most evanescent and evocative of the senses. A person suffering from cognitive impairment may not remember what she had for lunch, but, with one sniff of a rose, can relate every detail of her wedding some 60 years earlier.

The sense of smell plugs deep into the limbic system (the part of the brain that governs behavior, emotions and memory) as well as the cortex (home of conscious thought). Early scent memories are especially powerful—one whiff of Scotch pine and I'm back in my childhood home putting Christmas decorations on the tree. In an article exploring odor, Maxine Wilke writes that her sister "maintains she married her husband because he smelled exactly like the plastic Peter Pan doll of her childhood."[6]) As with color, culture and personal history enormously influence what smells we swoon or gag over. One person may adore the scent of lilies while another may find them repugnant because of an association with funerals. (Wilke says that "the only universally pleasant smell is cola, which explains the global success of Coke and Pepsi."[7])

Humans can distinguish 10,000 aromas through some 10 million sensory neurons and a region in the brain called the *olfactory bulb*. This may seem impressive but pales compared to most other creatures: the beagles trained to sniff out food and plants in airport luggage can detect a can of meat wrapped in plastic inside a sweater inside a suitcase on the baggage carousel, while the male emperor moth can detect the scent of a female moth 3.1 miles (5 km) away.

Flowers are only part of the garden's olfactory picture. Think of the smell of newly turned earth, the freshness of the air after a rain, the tang of cedar, or the sharp sweetness of rosemary. There's also the airborne calling card of a disgruntled skunk or the reek of a compost pile gone bad. (Nature is kind in a way: as we age, we become less sensitive to bad smells.) But even unpleasant smells are important (alerting us to possible danger, for instance, that food has gone off) and better than nothing—people who lose their sense of smell completely can become severely depressed.

Flower petals' scent comes from oils which evaporate forming volatile compounds—an orchid may have a hundred of these oils. Again, it comes down to sex and what pollinator they are trying to lure. Butterfly-pollinated flowers such as buddleja, lilies, phlox and milkweed, and bee-pollinated blooms such as snapdragons, clover and many fruits have a light, sweet fragrance. Beetle-pollinated flowers such as magnolias, dogwoods and wild roses have a strong fruity or spicy scent (and in some cases like skunk cabbage, a smell of fermentation). Moth-pollinated flowers such as nicotiana, Easter lily, datura, moonflower and yucca

Many butterfly-pollinated lilies are sweetly fragrant, but some have a heavier scent that can be overwhelming, especially indoors.

Aromatherapy Growing Guide

For Relaxation	For Revitalization	For Creating Balance	For Relieving Depression
Chamomile (*Chamaemelum*)	Angelica (*Angelica*)	Basil (*Ocimum basilicum*)	Angelica (*Angelica*)
Clary sage (*Salvia sclarea*)	Basil (*Ocimum basilicum*)	Lavender (*Lavandula*)	Basil (*Ocimum basilicum*)
Hops (*Humulus*)	Citrus (*Citrus*)	Rose (*Rosa*)	Carnation (*Dianthus*)
Juniper (*Juniperus*)	Eucalyptus (*Eucalyptus*)	Scented geranium (*Pelargonium*)	Chamomile (*Chamaemelum*)
Lemon balm (*Melissa officinalis*)	Fennel (*Foeniculum*)	Valerian (*Valeriana*)	Citrus (*Citrus*)
Marjoram (*Origanum*)	Jasmine (*Jasminum*)	Violet (*Viola*)	Clary sage (*Salvia sclarea*)
	Peppermint (*Mentha* x *piperita*)	Yarrow (*Achillea*)	Jasmine (*Jasminum*)
	Pine (*Pinus*)		Lavender (*Lavandula*)
	Rose (*Rosa*)		Rose (*Rosa*)
	Rosemary (*Rosmarinus*)		Scented geranium (*Pelargonium*)
	Thyme (*Thymus*)		

are night-bloomers with a heady, penetrating scent. And the fly-pollinated flowers are usually umbels (Queen Anne's lace) or composites (daisies) that have a mildly unpleasant odor.

Many plants also have scented leaves, bark, roots and even seeds. For some, this is a defense against getting browsed or munched; for others, it is a form of air-conditioning as the strong volatile compounds create a cooling layer around the leaves. "The old English custom of covering brick walls with sprigs of rosemary for cooling has been supported by modern research. Rosemary has 74 times the cooling effect of fresh air, while thyme has 68 times and lavender 60 times."[8]

The ability of fragrance to affect our mood and behavior underlies what is called *aromatherapy* (see above). The cosmetic industry has long promoted the powers of perfume, and it has spread to the workplace, as studies have shown that, for example, proofreaders worked better with lavender or peppermint scents infusing their environment. The difficulty with many commercial applications is that, since it is so expensive to obtain natural essential oils (it takes 4.5 million jasmine petals to produce about a pound /454 g of jasmine oil, for example), synthetic, chemical-laden products are used, the safety of which is a source of debate. Some people with

Favorite Fragrant Plants

Daphne (*Daphne*)

Magnolia (*Magnolia*)

Sweet pea (*Lathyrus odoratus*)

Scented geraniums, especially mint and nutmeg (*Pelargonium* spp.)

Viburnum, especially Korean spice (*Viburnum*, especially *V. carlesii*)

Datura (*Datura*)

Tree peonies (*Paeonia suffruticosa*)

Nicotiana (*Nicotiana alata*—the tall one; the short bushy types have little scent)

David Austin roses (*Rosa*)

allergies find even the natural but heavy scent of lilies or gardenias too much. (For more on respiratory allergies, see Chapter 12.)

Fragrant Tips

Plant fragrant flowers where you will enjoy them most: along a path or around a seating area. But stick to four or five types of scent in one area, or you risk olfactory overload. Fragrance varies with the time of day: roses are best in the morning and peak at noon, while nicotiana doesn't release its oils until twilight. Small fragrant plants are best grown in raised beds or containers so you don't have to grovel to get a whiff.

Taste

Taste is inseparable from the sense of smell. Thousands of taste buds on the tongue register four sensations—sweet, salty, sour and bitter— and a fifth called *umami,* which is savoury. The rest of the flavor comes from the aroma, as well as from the sensations provided by the food's texture (the celery's crunch), temperature (chili, ice cream) and appearance (raspberry red).

Not surprisingly, food taste and smells are also tremendously evocative. Look at Proust's famous mouthful of tea-soaked madeleine that summoned up his childhood, his aunt, her house, indeed the entire town. More recently, Yale University researchers found that the scent of spiced apples reduced stress and panic attacks in some people; another study found that claustrophobics were helped by the smell of cucumber; and New York's Sloan-Kettering Cancer Center uses the fragrance of vanilla to relax patients during treatment.[9]

A fetus acquires taste buds at the age of seven or eight weeks and they are functioning by the seventh month.[10] Apparently, that's when we also acquire a sweet tooth (metaphorically speaking). As adults, our tastes vary a great deal, especially in our sensitivity to bitter flavors such as grapefruit juice or espresso. Around 60, though, we start losing some of our sense of taste and smell, through normal aging, medications, illness and even pollution.

Obviously, the best taste candidates for any gardener are homegrown vegetables, fruits and herbs. Grown organically and eaten fresh, their taste will revive any flagging palate (see Chapters 8 and 9). But don't ignore other, more unusual edibles. We have many ways to battle weeds but eating them hasn't been on top of the list. In fact, some weeds are extremely nutritious. Lamb's quarters (*Chenopodium album*) contains iron, protein, vitamins B$_2$ and C and calcium and makes a great spinach substitute. Other vitamin-and-mineral-rich tastes of the wild include:

- Purslane (*Portulaca oleracea*) has a cool citrusy green flavor. Use leaves and tender stems, raw or cooked.
- Dandelion (*Taraxacum officinale*) can be used in salads. Pick young leaves before it goes to flower. Older leaves can be boiled, sautéed or braised.
- Chickweed (*Stellaria media*) is best when you use the young leaves.
- Chicory (*Cichorium intybus*) leaves can be used raw or cooked.

Obviously, any weeds you eat should be free of herbicides. Seeds for cultivated purslane (*Portulaca oleracea* var. *sativa*) and dandelions, with bigger, more tender leaves are available in some catalogs.

Floral Edibles

Chefs might have gone a bit overboard with this in recent years, but edible flowers add a rainbow of flavors and colors to pique the appetite.

Tips

- Don't eat flowers from florists, garden centers or roadsides.
- Pick the flowers in the early morning when the dew is off, wash gently and pat dry.
- Tiny flowers can be eaten whole, but eat only the petals of larger ones: remove stamens, pistils, any green parts and the white portion at the base of petals such as roses.
- Flowers/petals can be sprinkled over salads, crystallized for decoration or frozen in ice cubes, as well as used in sauces, preserves, vinegars and fritters.

Edible Flower Sampler

Borage (*Borago officinalis*)	Its blue flowers have a sweet flavor.
Pot marigold (*Calendula officinalis*)	Bright yellow and orange petals add zip to a salad.
Geraniums (*Pelargonium*)	Flowers and scented geranium leaves can be used.
Lavender (*Lavandula*)	Use finely chopped in salads.
Nasturtium (*Tropaeolum majus*)	Flowers and leaves are edible, and the seeds can be pickled as a caper substitute.
Pansy (*Viola wittrockiana*)	Use for their lovely colors.
Rose (*Rosa*)	All varieties can be used, though some may be too scented.
Violets (*Viola odorata*)	These are a favorite for crystallizing.

Sound

One summer we were working away in the garden, so absorbed in our earthy labors that we really didn't pay attention to the mixed chorus of sparrows, chickadees, robins, cardinals and the occasional shriek of insult from a blue jay—until it stopped, as abruptly as the flick of a switch. We both looked around in the sudden uncanny silence, trying to figure out what had happened. Then my husband pointed to the sky. High above us, drifting languidly on the air currents, were three hawks. We watched motionless as they wrote ever larger circles in the sky, eventually disappearing behind a ragged row of tall spruce trees.

Sometimes, we forget that a landscape is a soundscape, too. But isn't harmony an element of sound and also of a healing space where we go to resolve dissonance in our lives, thoughts and emotions? To hear waves breaking on a beach or wind whispering through the leaves, is to hear natural harmonic sounds that resonate deeply within us. Ross Barrable, maker of wind harps and sound gardens writes, "Listening with focused attention to harmonic sound has the capacity to stop the incessant, internal run of the mind. This quality of sound can draw the attention if only for a moment, to rest on an inner stillness that holds a depth of peace, not normally experienced in the outer world."[11]

We don't all live close to the ocean's watery heartbeat, but we can definitely bring the sound of water into our gardens, be it gentle bubbling or rushing cascade. (For more on the role of water in the garden, see Chapter 3.) That, in turn, brings the birds, with their trills and peeps; frogs add their bass notes; with a tiny whir, a bejewelled dragonfly lands on the warm waterside rock. Around our pond are some aralias (*Aralia*) whose extravagant leaves droop tropically in summer turning it into a sort of grotto (at least in my fanciful view). In August, they put out masses of tiny creamy flowers which are alive with bees—it's like being under an umbrella of humming pleasure.

Add additional notes to your garden tone poem with wind chimes or bells, paths of crunchy gravel and restless ornamental grasses. Hearken to the constant rustle of leaves—the great gardener, Gertrude Jekyll, who was practically blind, found that every tree has a distinctive song. Or take a lesson from tropical gardeners: grow large-leaved plants such as cannas (*Canna*) or petasites (*Petasites*) near a window or gazebo, so you can hear the rain drumming out endless improvisations on them.

The Wind Harp

Hear the music of the spheres with an Aeolian harp (or wind harp). Named for Aeolus, the Greek god of the winds, it is traditionally a wooden sound box loosely strung with 10 or 12 gut strings. All tuned to the same pitch, they resonate in the wind to different harmonic chords. Ross Barrable, a Canadian now living in Colorado, creates modern wind harps of materials such as bronze, titanium and stainless steel using the principles of sacred geometry. Alone, or arranged in a carefully designed sound garden, these elegant acoustical sculptures bring the harmonies of earth, wind and sky to our ears.

But of course, not all sounds are pleasant—noise is a problem even in rural areas. Sound is heard as vibrations or waves of sound pressure travel through the air to our ears where tiny cilia or receptors then transmit signals to the brain, which interprets and creates meaning out of them. It usually becomes noise when the intensity, measured as decibels, exceeds comfort level (though even low-level sounds can be extremely irritating). Two people talking normally registers about 65 decibels, a vacuum cleaner 75 decibels and a car horn 100 decibels. A pig squeal can hit 115 decibels and a jet engine 140 decibels.[12]

Some of the worst offenders are the machines created to cut trees, blow leaves and mow lawns. A chainsaw in action produces 116 decibels; a gas-powered blower 110–112 decibels; and a power mower 95–120 decibels. All are louder than a bulldozer (93–96 decibels) and even a jack hammer (102–111 decibels).[13]

It's even more shocking when you realize that each 10-decibel increase represents a tenfold increase in intensity, i.e., 40 decibels is 100 times more intense than 20 decibels. Physical pain for humans begins at 130 decibels, though prolonged exposure to noise levels of 85 decibels can result in permanent damage.

Noise pollution can cause irritability, fatigue, sleeplessness (the average person cannot sleep with noise above 45 decibels), stress, increased blood pressure, tinnitus, ulcers, heartburn and indigestion. And one burst of noise, from a passing truck, say, not only makes you jump out of your skin, it also alters endocrine, neurological and cardiovascular functions.[14]

So if you live near a noisy street (85 decibels), or there's construction close by (a 20-ton truck, 88 decibels), you want to try to screen that noise out. As outlined in Chapter 4, trees and shrubs are good sound barriers, especially if planted on an earth berm. And the pleasing sounds you create in your garden help to mask the unwanted sounds outside it.

Gas-powered machines are not only noisy, they are also major contributors to air pollution. I realize that for gardeners of considerable land, tractors, bushhogs and whatnot are labor-saving necessities. But, for most of us, raking instead of

A weathered bell brings a distinctive note to the garden soundscape.

blowing leaves is better exercise. The new reel mowers are lighter and more efficient; electric mowers are quieter by half and non-polluting. And perhaps that tree really doesn't need taking down at all. As Roger Swain reminds us, the Amish have a phrase for this kind of gardening—they say, "We are the quiet on the land."

Touch

I defy anyone to walk by some feathery artemisia (*Artemisia*) or a pot of woolly thyme (*Thymus*) and not stroke them. In one of my planter boxes is a little sign my mother gave me that reads: *Please Touch the Herbs.* We need more *please touch* signs about.

Exposed to constant stimulation, the skin is the body's largest organ and one of the most sensitive. In just .155 square inch (1 cm^2) of skin are 3 million cells, four yards (3.6 m) of nerves, one yard (.9 m) of blood vessels and 100 sweat glands. Within those four yards (3.6 m) of nerves are five different types of nerve endings, sensitive to heat, cold, pain, itch and pressure.[15] So while I have my hands in the soil, the back of my neck is feeling the warmth of the sun, my leg is registering a mosquito's bite and my arm is feeling the wayward branch pressing against me.

I recall reading about a little boy who was given a rose to smell at the Perkins School for the Blind in Watertown, Massachusetts. But instead of pushing his nose into the flower, he ever so slowly ran the petals across his lips. From the time we are born, we need to be touched. While most of the research deals with human touch, non-human touch can still have a potent affect—look at how much we love to stroke our pets and how much they love to be petted. Just as we can observe a lot by watching, so we can feel a lot by touching.

Getting in Touch
Soft and Furry Plants

The tactile possibilities in the garden could keep your hands busy for months. Put irresistibly touchable plants within easy reach, and less approachable ones at a safe remove.

- Lambs' ears (*Stachys byzantina*) are silvery, low-growing and perfectly named.
- Mint-scented geranium's (*Pelargonium tomentosum*) plush velvet leaves are headily fragrant (*tomentosum* means "hairy," so watch for plants with that word in their names).

- Pussy willow (*Salix discolor*) ushers in spring with its little furry "paws."
- Silver sage (*Salvia argentea*) has huge leaves covered in shimmery down.
- Love lies bleeding (*Amaranthus*), a Victorian floozy, sports rather bizarre flower tassels resembling chenille.

Plants with Smooth, Shiny Leaves or Bark
- Bergenia (*Bergenia cordifolia*) boasts glossy green leaves that turn red in fall.
- Japanese cherry (*Prunus serrula*) has chestnut bark that shines even more with regular rubbing.
- European ginger (*Asarum europaeum*), a low spreader, will get you on your hands and knees to give its small lustrous leaves a stroke.

Plants with a Feathery Feel
- Artemisias, especially 'Silvermound' (*A. schmidtiana*), have pungent gray-green foliage.
- Plumosa cockscombs (*Celosia*) sprout fluorescent spikes that feel downier than any flower should.

Low-growing, silvery lambs' ears (Stachys byzantina) *are perfectly named; children delight in their velvety feel.*

- Feather grass (*Stipa tenuissima*) and the aptly named squirrel-tail grass (*Hordeum jubatum*) are among many ornamental grasses with tactile flowers (inflorescences).

Plants with Textured Leaves

- Hostas (*Hosta*) put out mounds of thick, wrinkled, seersucker leaves (all the better to deter slugs).
- Bog-loving rodgersias' (*Rodgersia*) foliage has a hairy, slightly prickly texture.
- Bamboo's (*Pleioblastus*) distinctive leaves feel as soft as beagles' ears if you rub them one way and like fine sandpaper rubbed the opposite way.

Flowers with Sensual Silky Petals

- Magnolia—both star and saucer. I have it on good authority that the garden fairies sew these petals together for their gowns.
- Rose—the sheen queen of petals. The ancient Romans used to shower rose petals on their dinner guests.
- Tree peony—Their huge frilly petals are like a cross between silk and the finest Japanese paper; fragrant, too, they smell like fresh bread to me.
- Lilies—Their heavy petals are like some rich satin brought back over the ancient spice road.
- Poppies—Looking for all the world like crepe paper, they actually feel like cool, smooth velvet.

Plants with an Edge

- Conifers—the leaves aren't called needles for nothing, but yews (*Taxus*), firs (*Abies*) and false cypress (*Chamaecyparis*) are all friendly to the touch. Other trees such as the paperbark maple (*Acer griseum*) have peeling or ridged bark.
- Purple coneflower (*Echinacea*) is adored by flower arrangers; the cone part resembles a small hedgehog.
- Beech nuts (*Fagus*) have round, spike-covered casings like oversized burrs.
- Sweet woodruff's (*Galium odoratum*) seeds are like tiny balls of Velcro and form a ready attachment to all items of clothing.
- The horse chestnut's (*Aesculus hippocastanum*) smooth "conker," walnuts (*Juglans*), hickories (*Carya*), poppy (*Papaver*) seed heads, and lotus (*Nelumbo*) pods are among many tactile nuts and seeds.

Perilous Plants

Exercise caution around really prickly plants such as cardoon (*Cynara*), thistles (*Onopordon* and *Cirsium*), prickly pear cactus (*Opuntia*), sea holly (*Eryngium*), and such thorny plants as rose (*Rosa*), aralia (*Aralia*), five-fingered aralia (*Acanthopanax*) and barberry (*Berberis*). Some plants can cause a skin rash, so wear gloves when handling them:

- The euphorbia family including spurge and poinsettia; the white sap called *latex* is an irritant.
- Rue's (*Ruta graveolens*) foliage can induce a rash.
- Juniper's (*Juniperus*) needles and pollen can causes rashes.
- Stinging nettles (*Urtica dioica*) can give a ferocious "bite" if grabbed inadvertently.
- Poison ivy (*Toxicodendron radicans*) and poison oak (*T. pubescens*) grow in wilder areas. Remember the catch phrase, "leaves of three, let it be."

By attuning all our senses—from touch to sight—to the garden's vibrant life, we not only reap the sensory rewards but also hone the ancient skills of "reading" nature. Once again, we see significance in the bend of a grass stalk or the tiny holes in a leaf; hear the messages of rain and wind; taste a fruit's sourness that tells us the soil needs attention; smell the richness of well-made compost and feel the reassuring smoothness of a hosta leaf growing flush and fat. With our awareness heightened and curiosity thus aroused, we search for greater insight, and, in the process, grow as both gardeners and guardians of nature.

All members of the euphorbia family have a white sap called latex, which causes skin irritation in some people.

The Sky's the Limit

The skin of the city can be transformed into a living landscape.

THE LONDON ECOLOGY UNIT, 1993

High above the streets of downtown Vancouver, the wind ruffles a blue and green tapestry of grasses, stitched through with a ribbon of bearberry. In San Bruno, California, birds flock to undulating meadows of wildflowers, scarcely aware of the comings and goings of office workers beneath them. In Toronto, a senior's residence sprouts beans, tomatoes, cosmos and marigolds where once there was only gravel punctuated by air vents.

These three sites, the Vancouver Public Library, The Gap headquarters and the Baycrest Terrace, are all part of an approach that is greening some of the vast expanses of unclaimed, unused space in our cities: roofs. The green-roof movement is well rooted in Europe—in France in 1923, Le Corbusier built them into his designs, and today in parts of Switzerland and Germany, new industrial buildings are required by law to duplicate on their roofs the landscape they have replaced.[1] In North America, the movement is still at the seedling stage, but it is growing— and growing more vital as a way of making our cities healthier places to live and work. Groups in cities such as Portland, Oregon; Chicago, Illinois; Atlanta, Georgia; Ottawa and Toronto, Ontario, are marshalling resources and information, implementing pilot projects and generally banging the drum for greening our urban roofs.

Rooftop Greening

These green oases can be either carefully tended gardens full of ornamentals and vegetables (roof gardens) or simply a look-but-don't-touch roof covering of tough, low-maintenance and beautiful plants (green roofs). Both kinds carry tremendous environmental, ecological, economic and social benefits for city-dwellers and the larger world.

Saving Rain

As discussed in Chapter 3, the loss of rainwater as more and more land gets swallowed by the "proverbial asphalt jungle" is seriously overloading storm-water pipes that overflow into sewer systems and pollute our lakes and rivers. Watertight roofs full of vegetation can absorb from 75 to 100 per cent of the rain that falls on them in summer.[2] The plants take it up and, in transpiration, release it back into the atmosphere; what they don't use runs off gradually and is filtered en route as heavy metals such as cadmium and lead are bound in the soil.

Air Cleaning

Trees work mighty hard to clean our air, but the shrinking urban forest is no match for the vast amounts of pollution our fossil-fuel burning spews out. Acres of green roofs would provide the trees with welcome reinforcements—scooping up their share of carbon monoxide, sulfur dioxide, etc., and, of course, taking in carbon dioxide for photosynthesis and giving off oxygen. They'd also act as sky-borne Dustbusters, clearing the air of dust, ash, pollen and smoke. Just one square yard (.8 m^2) of grass on a roof can remove more than 5.3 ounces (150 grams) of particulates a year.[3]

Heating and Cooling

As asphalt and concrete soak up heat during the day, releasing it only slightly at night, our cities become hot spots or urban heat islands. The more trees and green roofs we have, the more the effect will be moderated, as the plants give off water, increasing humidity and cooling the air. Even more significant is the effect on the buildings themselves. A green roof acts as an extra layer of insulation, keeping the building cooler in summer and warmer in winter (and quieter all year—in a busy city, every bit of sound insulation counts). In summer, a tar-and-gravel roof can reach an unbelievable 190 degrees F (88 degrees C). That same roof covered with grass would stay around 77 degrees F (25 degrees C).[4] A building covered in grasses and plants between eight and 16 inches (20 and 40 cm) high could retain up to 50 per cent of heat otherwise lost through a regular roof, resulting in substantial savings.[5]

Habitat and Biodiversity

Planned with an eye to creating plant communities, i.e., a diverse mix of plants, rooftops can become habitats for wildlife at a safe remove from many urban perils. With the restrictions of soil depth and the extremes of heat and wind, though, it's unrealistic to think they can replace natural ecosystems. Still, they can act as "stepping stones," linking other natural islands of green, and extending the corridors traveled by wildlife. As design consultant Linda Velasquez points out, studies in the

United States show that butterflies will visit gardens up to 20 stories high and birds up to 19 stories.[6] The good thing is that slugs probably won't.

Food Cities

Rooftop gardens provide the urban farmer with fresh produce conveniently close at hand (no mealy tomatoes trucked for miles). It seems the (veggie) plots are thickening everywhere you look, satisfying the craving for fresh organic vegetables, saving money and often making money as well. As a bonus, the growing season on a roof is a tad longer, despite the exposed conditions, because of the heat of the city. People are growing their own, and supplying food banks and local markets (as the Plant a Row, Grow a Row idea has spread). Groups such as The American Community Gardening Association, Urban Harvest in Toronto and City Farmer in Vancouver show what can be done on high and at ground level, and provide a wealth of advice and information.

Therapeutic and Aesthetic

How marvelous it would be to look out of your office window and see a patchwork quilt of greenery instead of a gray sea of gravel and concrete squares visited only by the occasional morose seagull. Such a view would afford office workers the chance to refresh their concentration, lower their blood pressure, reduce muscle tension and stress, and increase positive feelings (as shown in Roger Ulrich's studies—see Chapter 1). Surrounded by greenery, people might rediscover their ecological consciousness, since nature would be right there, and not out of sight, out of mind.

A covering of green can transform the ugly-duckling aesthetics of commercial buildings, especially the endlessly drab rectangular boxes clustered in industrial malls. Roof greening gives architects and landscape architects a whole new dimension to work with to enhance a building's looks, value and efficiency. Urban hospitals often have nowhere to go but up, and are discovering that roof gardens can provide healing spaces for patients and their families, as well as staff members.

Building Community

Roof gardens grow friendships and enrich the social fabric, too. As Monica Kuhn writes, "Residents of apartment buildings who never meet in the halls, exchange seeds and stories in their roof gardens; children who cannot play on the street below now play on the roofs above." [7]

Before You Get Growing

So you're all gung-ho on the idea of a roof garden—but do some homework before you start ordering stacks of planters, tons of soil, yards of decking and armloads of plants. There are some weighty considerations—literally. All this stuff is heavy, as anyone who has tried to move a tree with even a small root ball knows. Wet soil weighs 100 pounds per cubic foot (45.3 kg per .03 m³); just a gallon (3.8 L) of water weighs about eight pounds (3.6 kg). Most roofs are designed for a load of only 40 pounds per cubic foot (18 kg per .03 m³), so be sure you know your roof's structure and consult a professional engineer to see what reinforcment might be necessary.[8] Roof gardens don't need huge amounts of soil and you can use lighter soilless mixes, or rockwool products (the kind used in hydroponic gardening).

Besides weight, you need to consider water. Obviously, you want to make the most of rainwater and avoid having to schlep water up to the roof, so having a water

Enclosed in greenery and protected from wind and sun, this rooftop/ balcony garden makes the most of pots and evergreen foliage.

source there is ideal. Check out the various waterproof membrane systems now available, taking into account what exists already on the roof. Drainage is crucial. Filter cloths will prevent soil loss and keep the drains from clogging. Check local bylaws or city ordinances regarding safety issues, perimeter fencing, etc.

Choose plants that don't send down deep tap roots, and that can withstand wind, sun, drought and air pollution. Grasses, sedums (*Sedum*), hens and chicks (*Sempervivum*), and irises (*Iris*) are tough enough customers, but in ornamental settings with arbors, lattice windbreaks, and/or shade from other buildings, you can look to small trees, shrubs, evergreens, perennials, annuals and herbs. The sky's the limit. Containers with perennials or shrubs should be lined with Styrofoam for winter protection. And don't use terracotta pots; there are fabulous lightweight look-alikes made of fiberglass and plastic that will winter over without cracking.

Under Glass

Given the long winters of the northern states and Canada, Wisconsin architect Roald Gundersen proposes another option: a sustainable, solar greenhouse designed for rooftop use in cold climates. Rooftop greenhouses could be used to grow food and flowers year-round, and, while they don't vacuum up pollution, they can provide just as much insulation value to the building. And they bring the outside in. "We spend 94 per cent of our time indoors, yet all things in a building are dead," says Gundersen. "Greenhouses offer the potential to take us back to the human ecology we lost… when we entered the industrial age."[9]

Community Gardening

Urban agriculture's grass roots have largely been at ground level in community gardens across the country. Historically, perhaps the best known were the railway gardens (1890–1930) set up by the Canadian Pacific Railway to beautify local stations all along the line. Thousands of people got busy planting relief gardens during the First World War and victory gardens during the Second World War, growing food for themselves and the war effort.[10]

Community gardens can be "a powerful antidote to hunger, poverty, loneliness and cultural isolation."[11] They bring people together to share knowledge, tools and materials, not to mention recipes for zucchini (one can never have too

many—recipes, that is). Fostering a sense of community is what it's all about, people caring for their neighborhood—and neighbors—and making a real difference in what could otherwise be an impersonal, bleak environment.

Urban farmers can feed themselves and make some money selling produce, herbs or flowers—whatever, especially if they grow unusual or heritage varieties not readily available. And they get all the benefits of exercise, fresh air, interaction with nature, social contact and a sense of community empowerment. These green pockets confer the same ecological benefits as rooftop gardens by zapping pollution, saving rainwater, cooling the heat island and providing a beautiful oasis of restorative greenery.

It's well known that establishing a community garden can be a giant step in restoring run-down neighborhoods—motivating people to care, drawing young and old together to clean up and get growing. I visited an exuberant community garden on Chicago's South Side and was told that the first year, the organizers got 30 or so children involved but couldn't attract the adults. So they sent each child home with some unfamiliar vegetable and a note pinned to his or her shirt reading, "To

Oases of green growth in the city, community gardens bring people together to share knowledge, laughter and tools, not to mention recipes for zucchini.

learn how to cook this, call this number...." The organizers figured few parents could resist their child's plea to prepare such carefully tended, precious produce. It worked. The following year, the project had double the attendance—and all the new people were adults. Green thumbs are contagious. All around the neighborhood were window boxes, pots of annuals and circles of impatiens around practically every tree.

The garden was enclosed by a low, easily scaled fence. "What about vandalism?" the organizers were asked. The first year, they had enlisted a couple of the toughest kids in the area to act as "policemen" so that solved that. Two large baskets hung outside the gate were kept filled with veggies for people to help themselves, so there was little theft, just great towers of beans, tomatoes and okra, mounds of squash and cauliflower, and ferny waves of carrot tops, and over it all a thrumming of busy insects and the sweet smell of success.

These gardens, like much else we have explored, have a ripple effect. As William Rees explains in his article, *"Why Urban Agriculture?"*, the increase in locally grown food can reduce the amount of food-related trucking; fewer trucks on the road mean fewer pollutants being generated. Fresh produce carried a short distance in a paper bag or reusable basket saves packaging, refrigeration, preservatives and shipping costs.[12] Composting and organic growing practices (recycling newspapers as mulch and plastic bottles as cloches and bird feeders, for example) reduce the amount of garbage going to landfills, save water and avoid the cost and pollution of chemical pesticides and fertilizers.

Naturalization in Schools

If you were lucky as a child, you grew up somewhere near a "wild" area. I recall being drawn like a magnet to the edge of a forbidden "swamp." It probably wasn't a full-fledged swamp but it was big enough for us, full of green algae and fascination. Bullrushes (*Typha*) stood guard at the edges and we spent hours trying to catch tadpoles, while dragonflies dove about like iridescent UFOs. I was also lucky enough to have woods nearby, too, which in spring were like a pale green cathedral, carpeted with white trilliums (*Trillium*).

In their evocative book, *The Geography of Childhood*, Gary Nabhan and Stephen Trimble capture how vital it is for children to have contact with nature, to experience their own wilderness. As nearly 40 per cent of the world's population is urbanized, children grow up in a world of asphalt, concrete, glass and steel. Worse, the average North American child spends only three hours a week in active play, compared to 27 hours in front of the TV and countless more in front of a computer.

"As children, we need time to wander, to be outside, to nibble on icicles and watch ants, to build with dirt and sticks in a hollow of the earth, to lie back and contemplate clouds and chickadees. These simple acts forge the connections that define a land of one's own—home and refuge.... With these childhood experiences we begin. They form the secure foundation to which we return again and again in our struggle to be strong and connected, to be complete."[13]

In addition to natural place spaces in the home garden, another obvious place where these early bonds with nature can be forged is at school. Early in this century, school gardens flourished as part of a nature-study movement that saw every child with a little plot in which to grow flowers and vegetables from seed.[14] Today's schoolyard, where the average North American child by the end of the sixth grade will have spent approximately 260 full days, is often a brick wall with a half-dead cedar or two facing expanses of beaten grass and dusty asphalt. This is a bleak environmental message if ever there was one. (Even worse, in summer, these surfaces act like mini heat-islands.)

But school playgrounds are changing, thanks to organizations like the National Gardening Association in the United States and Evergreen in Canada. School grounds (along with rooftops) offer great untapped potential for naturalizing, the ideal habitat for learning. Schools which have enlisted the greatest teacher

Real Neighborly

The kind of social action that blooms with gardening is typified by Neighbourgardens, a not-for-profit group started by Rae Blewden in Vancouver that connects people who have garden space but lack the knowledge, ability or time to tend it with people who do have the time, ability and knowledge but no place to use them. People from all cultures are matched, as well as young gardeners with old (resulting in a whole lot of invaluable hort know-how being passed on), able-bodied with those with disabilities, and so on in a continuous learning and growing process that builds friendships and enriches both the participants and the land.

there is—nature—have found their students performed better in math, social studies and science, and developed better interpersonal skills, self-discipline, camaraderie and respect for each other and the earth. Currently, over a three-year period in Canada, Evergreen is actively involving 500,000 Canadian students, and will educate 6.3 million more in programs designed to transform their barren school grounds.

While school natural landscapes are important, it is just as important that children understand that their garden is just one piece in the natural jigsaw puzzle. Interpretive naturalist and co-author of a manual about schoolyard naturalization, Henry Kock suggests establishing a tree nursery: the children start the trees from seed and tend them from year to year, so there is continuity and a sense of ownership. By the time the children graduate, the trees can be transplanted—out into the community, where the child will see it become part of the local landscape.

Balcony and Doorstep Gardens

Whether you're in an apartment on the second floor or the twentieth, in a rowhouse or a rooming house, there's always room for a garden. On my first trip to Denmark, I remember being struck by the apartment buildings absolutely festooned with flowers. Every balcony, every iron railing sported boxes, grow-bags and/or hanging baskets overflowing with color. And it wasn't just one building; it was every building!

Gardening on high does present certain challenges. Balconies are often either terrifically bright or permanently gloomy. North-facing balconies get the least sun, so you'll probably have to abandon any dreams of giant tomatoes smothered with your own fresh basil. But there are still rich possibilities in annuals, perennials, small shrubs and some veggies. Here are some ideas for making the most of your high-rise plot.

Use lattice panels with vines or perhaps or tall ornamental grasses as a wind break. Your containers should be lightweight (as with roofs, balconies can only take so much weight) and filled with soilless mix. You can use funky, recycled containers such as old washtubs or orange crates to add personality. Grow-bags are excellent if you have a means to hang them up since they don't dry out as quickly as most containers.

When watering, be careful that you're not raining on a lower resident's parade. Place the containers on pot feet and put an extra drainage tray underneath to catch run-off. Don't let the pots sit in the water though or the roots will rot. If you're using window boxes and hanging baskets, make sure they are securely fastened, and, again, watch the water so you don't give someone an unexpected shower. Adding water-retaining polymers and slow-release fertilizer to your potting mix at planting time will save feeding and watering. Mulch also helps, but if the containers are densely planted, it isn't as vital. If you have an electrical outlet, get a small recirculating pump, a bowl and some rocks and set up a little water feature; it will add immeasurably to the verdant feeling and also help to mask the traffic noise below. Or think bigger and make a pond in a barrel, large pot or even a recycled bathtub. And don't forget to make enough room for a comfy chair (or two) so you can relax and enjoy your private paradise.

Showing creative use of containers, this balcony pond in a recycled bathtub raises water-gardening to new heights.

Creating a Doorstep Garden

Turn a small space into a grand entry with a doorstep garden. Use every inch to create a varied plantscape from floor to ceiling. Frame the doorway with groupings of pots (squat, tall, round, plain, ornate), chock full of trailing plants as well as tall, sculptural ones. Stuff in plants such as nicotiana (*Nicotiana*), lavender (*Lavandula*), rosemary (*Rosmarinus*), thyme (*Thymus*), eucalyptus (*Eucalyptus*) or scented geraniums (*Pelargonium*) that will release their fragrance as people brush by. Put a trellis or lattice work on the walls to support vines, or hang more pots on. Think lush, lush, lush.

A riot of plants spilling over funky containers add life and color to an apartment doorway.

Farming in Pots

Balcony farmers must choose their crops carefully to enjoy a rich harvest. Many vegetables come in dwarf varieties or odd shapes and sizes that make them better suited to container growing. For instance, wee ball-shaped carrots such as 'Bolina' and 'Little Ball' beets.

Look for patio and cherry tomatoes such as 'Tiny Tim,' 'Hybrid Pixie Red' or the 'Red Pear' and 'Yellow Pear' which are shaped like little light bulbs. One plant per pot is plenty, though you can tuck in some basil and parsley alongside. Give them sun and consistent watering. Erratic dry/wet conditions will result in blossom end rot and other nasty things.

'Little Marvel' and 'Spring' peas grow a dainty 18 inches (45 cm) in height. They like cool weather but full sun and even moisture. Or plant a large bowl with mesclun mix. Constantly shearing the tender young leaves and reseeding will keep you in salad greens for weeks. Also try 'Lollo Rossa Red & Green,' a mini lettuce the size of a grapefruit, with lime-green leaves inside surrounded by red-splashed ones. You can also try some unusual peppers, such as 'Hybrid Fluo Violet,' a bright purple, or 'Hybrid Fluo Chocolate,' the color of darkest cocoa, but don't plant peppers out until nighttime temperatures are above 55 degrees F (13 degrees C).

Other veggies suitable for containers include 'Little Leaf' cucumber, which has as you might expect, small triangular leaves; it's very compact but very productive and is good for salads and for pickling. Oriental vegetables such as 'Hybrid Tatsoi,' 'Hybrid Green Boy,' and 'Hybrid Joi Choi' are compact and grow rapidly. Stems and leaves are edible and full of vitamins. And maybe you won't need quite so many zucchini recipes if you grow the perfectly round miniature, 'Hybrid Eight Ball.' This compact but open-growing plant likes a moist, organic soil and plenty of sun. Finally, for late-season harvest, why not grow a small-scale pumpkin such as 'Jack-B-Little' up a trellis? Make sure it has lots of organic matter and keep it well watered, and you'll have your own mini jack-o'-lantern decorations for Halloween.

The city farmer, the roof gardener and the enlightened builders of green roofs know they are restoring some of the urban green space that is rapidly being eaten up by development. Home to the majority of North Americans, cities are expanding their concrete and asphalt reach, sometimes until their boundaries meet and blend, creating a megalopolis such as the one extending from Boston to Washington, D.C. Increased urbanization and an even sharper split between city and country make urban "re-leaf" more vital than ever. Green efforts to reduce the noise, congestion, pollution and stress of our cities can work on every level—from ground to penthouse, from school to office tower, from practical to aesthetic, from human to environmental. To borrow natural gardening advocate Lorraine Johnson's phrase, "grow wild" in the city, and see what a difference it can make.

THE HEALTHY GARDENER

*What we tap into in our gardens
is not easily rationalized or explained,
but it's something we should never
have to give up.*

GENE ROTHERT,
*THE ENABLING GARDEN:
CREATING BARRIER-FREE GARDENS,* 1994

Ask gardeners why they garden and chances are they'll reply that it offers relief from stress, the stress of work, family pressures, the pace of daily activities, or private anxieties and fears. Stress is quite subjective (my stress could be your exhilaration) and varies in degree (from divorce to losing a prized hellebore) but one thing is certain: our health is closely related to how well we cope with it.

Stress is thought to be a factor in heart disease, diabetes, gastrointestinal disorders and high blood pressure, as well as depression, migraines, insomnia, alcoholism and drug abuse. It's also suspected that the stress hormones exacerbate bacterial infections and delay healing. So reducing stress can have a huge impact—boosting the body's natural defenses and thereby making it less vulnerable to illness, as well as improving one's sense of well-being, optimism and hope (in itself a health-enhancer).

The stress reduction that gardeners say they're hooked on has been confirmed by Texas A&M's Roger S. Ulrich, whose research showed that people recovered from stress faster and to a greater degree when exposed to natural settings as opposed to urban/built environments—often in less than five minutes.[1] And Japanese research has shown that viewing vegetation increases alpha waves in the brain, i.e., it has a relaxing effect. (See Chapter 1 for more on such studies.) Add to that the satisfaction of sowing and planting, nurturing and watering, with a bit of slug-bashing along the way, and it's no surprise that gardening is one of the fastest growing pastimes in North America.

Going hand in hand with stress is another plague of modern society, depression. It is the most common psychological problem in the United States, affecting more than 17.6 million people a year (and many more go undiagnosed). If the garden can help relieve stress, perhaps it can also help with depression. A study by Dr. James Blumenthal of Duke University Medical Center holds out hope. His subjects, all people suffering from depression, were divided into three groups: one doing half an hour of aerobic exercise three times a week; one taking antidepressant drugs, and one doing a combination of the two. After 16 weeks, all three had significantly lower levels of depression, leading Blumenthal to conclude that exercise was as effective as the drugs (the combination of the two had no greater impact). He noted, too, that the effects of the exercise program were much longer lasting; after a further six months, only 8 per cent of the exercising group relapsed into depression

Gardening Your Way Through Grief

So much of our emotional well-being depends on our ability to cope with loss. Whatever kind of loss—a loved one, a pet, a job, a home, a faculty (sight) or an ability (use of a knee, for instance)—we mourn and go through the grieving process. Nature has long been a part of that process and our rituals, from flowers to memorial gardens. But something called "grief gardening" goes far beyond that. In an AHTA Journal account, environmental horticulturist Elan Marie Miavitz describes the comfort she found planting pansies—she calls them *thera-pansies*—after her beloved father died. Discovering that gardening provides the release needed by people grappling with feelings they can't sort out, she started a grief gardening group. Her first group included half a dozen women who came for three-hour sessions over 12 weeks, spending the time planting dahlias, dividing daylilies and creating a bed of annuals.[3]

In nurturing living things, and fostering the continuity of life beyond themselves, they found relief from the physical symptoms of grief, as well as a deeper understanding of what garden writer Henry Mitchell calls "the great cycle of wheeling life." Afterwards, one participant wrote, "We have shared stories of our loved ones, learned valuable information about gardening, planted, weeded, read, cried, laughed and hugged." Wrote another, "I am going to take what I learned about using the soil as a symbol of life to continue to heal."

compared to 38 per cent of the drug group.[2] The subjects weren't gardening, but any gardener will tell you that half an hour of mowing, raking or digging is definitely a good workout. (See "Get Exercised" below.)

Get Exercised

Is gardening good exercise? The answer is yes. Especially if you put some effort into it and don't just putter about. More and more news reports lament the growing girth of North Americans, of all ages, so any regular exercise is beneficial. Ideally, we should expend 2,000 calories a week in activities outside our daily routines, and there are many ways of burning those up in the garden. Even relatively light work such as weeding, trimming or raking burns about 300 calories an hour. Digging, hauling mulch and heavier work not only burns calories but also improves muscle tone—and bone strength. This is not surprising when you consider a University of Arkansas study that revealed that women who gardened at least once a week had stronger bones than those who jogged, swam, walked or did aerobics. Gardening and weight training were called the "optimal choices" for maintaining bone density.[4] Added benefit came from being outside in the sunshine (vitamin D helps the body to absorb calcium).

The researchers at Duke University Medical Center have found that exercise does more than relieve depression—half an hour of aerobic exercise three times a week improved the cognitive abilities (memory, planning, juggling several tasks at once, etc.) of middle-aged and older people. Dr. Blumenthal, who published the findings in the *Journal of Aging and Physical Activity*, thinks exercise could improve the flow of oxygen-rich blood to the brain, resulting in better performance.[5] Getting that exercise in the garden surely beats jumping around in a gym or pounding out miles on a stationary bike. Plus, the more enjoyable the activity, the more motivated you are to keep doing it.

Activity, both physical and mental, also helps to ward off Alzheimer's disease, according to a study by Cleveland neurologist Dr. Robert Friedland. The study looked at the degree of participation in 26 different non-work activities including gardening and racquet sports (physical), watching TV and attending church (passive), and reading and playing a musical instrument (intellectual) for at least five years before the onset of Alzheimer's symptoms. "People who were less active were more than three times more likely to have Alzheimer's disease as compared to those who were more active," said Dr. Friedland.[6]

Getting the Most from Your Gardening Workout

Good sense should prevail when gardening as when doing any exercise.

- Warm up with some stretching before you start, especially in spring when your muscles are winter-stiff.
- Vary your activities and positions; weed for half an hour, then dig in compost, or replant a container or pick some flowers for an arrangement. Switch hands when doing repetitive tasks such as raking.
- Save your knees. Use a padded kneeler when possible, and stand up and stretch periodically.
- Save your back. When lifting, keep your back straight and bend your knees. Use lightweight tools and don't try to lift too much at once.
- Carry heavy pots or bags of soil close to your body to avoid back strain; better yet, use a small garden cart, or my favorite, a child's little red wagon.
- For the best workout, maintain a constant level of activity, instead of stopping and starting. Use manual tools instead of noisy power equipment.

Active Measures

This table shows exertion values assigned to various physical activities. The values were based on the ratio of the associated metabolic rate for the specific activity divided by the resting metabolic rate. Check out how much energy you are expending.

Effort Expended in Gardening Activities	Effort Expended in Other Activities
1.5 Watering lawn or garden, standing or walking	0.9 Lying quietly, reclining, sleeping
2.5 Applying fertilizer or seeding a lawn, walking	1.5 Sitting, knitting, sewing
3.5 Trimming shrubs or trees with a power cutter	2.3 Walking while shopping
4.0 Raking lawn, sacking grass and leaves; planting seeds and shrubs	3.0 Carpentry, general, workshop; bowling
4.5 Mowing lawn with a power mower; weeding, cultivating garden; planting trees; trimming shrubs or trees manually	3.5 Walking, 3.0 mph (4.8 kph), level, moderate pace, firm surface
	4.0 Bicycling
5.0 Carrying, loading or stacking wood; clearing land, hauling branches; laying sod	4.5 Cleaning, heavy or major; golf, general
	5.0 Softball or baseball, general; bicycling, stationary, general
6.0 Chopping wood, splitting logs; mowing lawn with hand mower; gardening with heavy power tools; tilling a garden; light (less than 10 lbs./4.5 kg per min.) shoveling	6.0 Aerobics, general; swimming, general
	7.0 Jogging, general[7]

It's thought that the brain stimulation associated with intellectual and physical activities works against the neurodegeneration of diseases such as Alzheimer's. Not surprisingly, watching TV did not lower the risk of Alzheimer's. The findings also suggest that it's never too late to get started, especially where intellectual activities are concerned.

Dr. Friedland may have classified gardening as physical, but—remember that sixth sense—it can be just as intellectually engaging: learning plant names, propagation techniques, botany, soil science, insect life cycles, color theory, garden design and so on. In fact, gardeners never stop learning. As Henry Kock is fond of saying, "There's more to nature than we know, and more than we *can* know."

The Sneeze-Free Garden

Sniff, sneeze, wheeze and sniffle. Thousands of people find going into the garden or even outdoors for any length of time difficult due to allergies. What makes people allergic? Part of it is hereditary; the rest is a misperception by your body as the immune system responds to what is essentially a false alarm. When a grain of pollen, for instance, lands for the first time inside the nose of an allergic person, instead of being taken down to the throat and swallowed or coughed out, it sets off a chemical reaction. The immune system treats it as an invader and produces large amounts of antibodies to fight that particular type of pollen. These antibodies attach themselves to tissue and blood cells. Any subsequent exposure to the same pollen then triggers the cells to produce powerful inflammatory chemicals such as histamine that result in the wretched respiratory allergy symptoms such as runny nose, sneezing, coughing and red, itchy, watering eyes. Sometimes these allergies can develop into asthma, which can be disabling and even fatal.

Pollen, produced by trees, grasses and other plants, is the most common allergen, followed by dust, molds and animal dander. As far as the plants go, pollen is all a matter of sex. These microscopic grains are produced by male plants (or parts of a plant) to fertilize the female plants (or parts thereof), resulting in flowers and fruit. Much pollination is done by insects that carry pollen from one plant to another as they forage for nectar (one of the plant's inducements to these sexual go-betweens).

Judged according to Thomas Ogren's allergy scale, this woodland garden gets a good report card. The hostas and heucheras are best with a rating of one (the lower the number, the lower the allergy quotient) while the hardy geraniums rate a 3. The rhododendrons fetch a 4, but their pollen is heavy so it falls rather than blowing, and is unlikely to be troublesome.

Allergy Planting Guide

Thomas Ogren has patiently rated hundreds of trees, shrubs, perennials and annuals for their allergy-causing potential on a scale of 1 to 10 (best to worst).

Ten of the Best Low-Allergy Plants	Ten of the Worst High-Allergy Plants
Coralbells (*Heuchera*)	Black ash (*Fraxinus nigra*)
Female junipers (*Juniperus scopulorum* and *J. virginiana*). Look for berries.	Castor bean (*Ricinus communis*)
	Chinese elm (*Ulmus parvifolia*)
Female red maple (*Acer rubrum*)	Fountain grass (*Pennisetum setaceum*)
Female white mulberry (*Morus alba*)	Japanese cedar (*Cryptomeria japonica*)
Female willows (*Salix*)	Japanese zelkova (*Zelkova serrata*)
Female yews (*Taxus*). Look for red berries.	Male fringe tree (*Chionanthus virginicus*)
Hosta (*Hosta*)	Male willows (*Salix*)
Impatiens (*Impatiens*)	Paper mulberry (*Broussonetia papyrifera*)
Johnny-jump-up (*Viola tricolor*)	Russian olive (*Elaeagnus angustifolia*)[9]
Vinca (*Catharanthus roseus*)	

But many trees and grasses, particularly those with insignificant flowers, cast their seed (so to speak) on the wind, relying on a stiff breeze to do the job. They are the real allergy-causing culprits. Light and dry, this pollen is produced in huge quantities (one ragweed can emit a million grains of pollen a day) and can be carried great distances. Samples of ragweed pollen have been gathered 400 miles (643 km) out at sea and 2 miles (3.2 km) up in the air.[8] Other weedy but powerful pollen producers are redroot pigweed (*Amaranthus retroflexus*), lamb's quarters (*Chenopodium album*) and English plantain (*Plantago lanceolata*). The major lawn or pasture grass culprits are Kentucky bluegrass (*Poa pratensis*), bent grass (*Agrostis*), timothy grass (*Phleum*) and orchard grass (*Dactylis*). Red fescue (*Festuca*) when kept mowed as a lawn is fine, but the blue fescues (*F. glauca*) and other ornamental grasses such as fountain grass (*Pennisetum*) are prolific pollen producers. Some trees such as pine (*Pinus*) also emit huge amounts of pollen but the grains are heavy and tend to fall quickly out of reach of the human nose.

We can't control the pollen flying in from distant parts, but we can certainly make our own backyards more allergy-free. Trees that are often listed as the major bad guys pollen-wise include ash (*Fraxinus*), elm (*Ulmus*), oak (*Quercus*), hickory (*Carya*), box elder (*Acer negundo*), maple (*Acer*) and mountain cedar (*Juniperus ashei*). But as Thomas L. Ogren argues in his commendable book, *Allergy-Free Gardening, The Revolutionary Guide to Healthy Landscaping*, it is a mistake to banish all such trees. Going back to sex again, Ogren points out that many trees are *dioecious* meaning there are separate male and female trees, as opposed to *monoecious* plants which possess male and female parts on the same plant. It is only the male dioecious trees that produce clouds of pernicious pollen; the females sedately produce only seeds and fruit, once pollinated. So, if we plant only the female maples or ashes, we will have less pollen pollution to contend with. The reason so many male trees are planted along streets and boulevards is because the flowers/fruits/seed from the females are deemed too "messy." This really is true in the case of the ginkgo (*Ginkgo biloba*), whose fruits are not only slimy but emit a revolting stench. But the female ginkgo won't cause allergies.

As far as monoecious plants go, some are severe allergy triggers, others less so. It depends more on where the flowers are situated. If, like corn, the pollen has merely to drop a short distance from the top of the plant to the flowers below, it is not likely to cause a problem. However, if, like the castor bean plant (*Ricinus communis*), the male flowers are at the bottom and the pollen must float up to the female parts, then watch out.

Other allergens are mold and spores. Avoid spore-producing ferns and plants such as phlox (*Phlox*) and bee balm (*Monarda*) that are prone to powdery mildew. Keeping plants healthy is key: sick plants attract disease and insects. Aphids, for example, produce honeydew, which in turn grows mold, and before you know it, there are a few million more airborne spores.

The heavy fragrances of flowers such as gardenia (*Gardenia*) and datura (*Datura*) can cause problems for some people. Paddy Wales, who took the gorgeous pictures in this book, laments that she can't go near 'Stargazer' lilies (*Lilium* 'Stargazer') or lavender (*Lavandula*).

To Reduce Pollen Exposure

- Avoid working outdoors in the early morning when pollen counts are highest (they are lowest in the middle of the day). Cool, cloudy, windless days are best, especially after a good rain.

Avoiding Stings and Bites

Natural gardeners work hard to attract insects and are pleased to see them buzzing and humming about. But some people are either frightened of them or can, when stung, suffer a severe allergic reaction to stings called *anaphylactic shock*.

- Place the bees' and wasps' favorite plants at the back of the border well away from paths and sitting areas. The critters will be more interested in the flowers than in you, but staying out of their flight paths just makes sense.

- Don't try to bat bees or wasps away with your hands—a friend of mine just waved her hand in animated conversation and was stung.

- Wear plain, light-colored clothing (no bright colors or floral patterns).

- Hold off on the perfume, scented cosmetics and deodorant, and rinse yourself off if you work up a sweat. Remember insects have an incredibly keen sense of smell.

- Keep any garbage containers or food covered tightly, and that includes fresh kitchen scraps on the compost pile. Stay away from orchards if there is a lot of rotting fruit on the ground. Food of any sort is especially popular with yellow jackets, which seem to be the most easily riled and can sting multiple times. I've found that bees are rarely perturbed unless you are aggressive toward them or the hive.

- If you are particularly sensitive to stings, carry an anaphylaxis kit containing epinephrine at all times.

- Keep your garden free of any standing water; even that little puddle on top of a bag of potting soil can be a breeding ground for mosquitoes.

- Encourage birds and bats which love mosquito hors d'oeuvres.

- Do *not* put up a bug zapper; those "blue-light specials" kill far more beneficial insects than mosquitoes.

A bee homes in on the flowers of a statuesque Nectaroscordum siculum. *Staying out of stinging insects' flight paths just makes good sense.*

- Wear a dust mask when mowing the lawn. Those with severe allergies are advised to use a respirator, as well as goggles. (Or take out of the grass completely and plant low-allergen groundcovers).
- Get rid of weeds before they flower.
- Choose insect-pollinated and low-allergy plants.

Sun

One of the great pleasures of working outside in the garden is the golden warmth of the sun. Sunlight is vital to our health in boosting vitamin D production, but, given ozone depletion and the rise in the rate of skin cancer, it's necessary to avoid over-exposure. Remember to cover up, wear a hat and always apply sunscreen. Be sure to drink lots of water on hot days. If you feel dizzy, stop what you're doing, rest in the shade and drink cool water, or raspberry or peppermint tea.

Gardening Made Easier

Much of the emphasis on gardening aids is geared toward our aging population, but "kids" in their thirties should be just as careful of their backs. Still, there are ways of making certain garden tasks easier, enabling everyone to garden longer.

Number one is probably raised beds. There are innumerable ways of building raised beds, from permanent structures made of brick, stone or wood, to A-frame or table-style planters that can be moved about or taken down. They can be any height that is comfortable but should be no more than five feet (1.5 m) across for easy access from both sides (30 inches/75 cm if access is only from one side). A wide coping on the top of the walls can double as seating, or provide support for someone with balance problems. Raised beds bring plants closer for observation and crops closer for harvesting, particularly for people using wheelchairs. Pathways should be generous (four to five feet/1.2 to 1.5 m wide) and level with an even, non-glare surface that doesn't get slick when wet. Gravel, turf and bark chips are too soft for wheelchairs.

There are many kinds of lightweight, ergonomically designed tools and other aids to make your gardening life easier. Hand tools with pistol grips are less strain on the wrist, while curved-handled rakes save your back. You can also get things such as D-grips to add to your existing long-handled tools, or padded foam cylinders to slip over handles—a great help for arthritis-sufferers. If bending is difficult, work from a padded stool. You can reach just as effectively with a lightweight extending-handle tool. Incorporate seating throughout the garden; there are all kinds of inventive designs, including planter/bench combos. Use a kneeler which has tubular metal side pieces (and doubles as a seat) or a sponge pad or knee pads to save wear and tear on your knees. Have hose bibs installed with your planters, put in a drip irrigation system and use wands or squeeze-type water bottles to save carting hoses or heavy watering cans. Put hand tools, twine, labels, whatever you need in a bucket and take it with you to avoid running back and forth to the shed or garage. Or use the aforementioned little red wagon, which can double as a seat. Finally, keep hanging baskets at a convenient height or use a pulley system for easy watering, deadheading, etc.

Down-to-earth plant choices and some labor-saving practices can make gardening more carefree. For containers, fill the bottom third with recycled Styrofoam popcorn, or crumpled plastic six-packs from annuals. It will add drainage and make the pots lighter. Put big containers on wheeled dollies to make them easier to move around. Use soilless potting mix in containers, with slow-release fertilizer and water-retaining polymers to save on watering. Whether for the border or containers, choose easy-care, non-invasive perennials that don't need frequent division. Use mixed shrub borders instead of hedges that need constant trimming, and look for native plants and cultivars that have good disease- and pest-resistance. You can get nature to do a lot of work for you: provide lots of organic matter and the worms will do the digging; bring birds into the garden to control pests; in dry areas, use drought-tolerant plants that won't need a lot of water; replace lawn with groundcover, and remember that magic word, mulch.

Just as you adapt your garden to your changing needs and abilities, so too is nature forever adapting. In fact, the only constant in the garden is change—with every season, every cycle of the moon and every round of the sun. The garden grows with you, and you grow with the garden in a mutual search for balance and serenity.

In the garden, as well as in our lives, even a small change can have surprisingly dramatic repercussions. As the principle popularly known as the "butterfly effect" has it, the flap of a butterfly's wing here can result in a hurricane on the other side of the world. This idea came out of studies in the 1970s by Edward Lorenz,

Garden Up

Grow plants up arbors, pergolas, obelisks, trellises and walls.

A piece of lattice and a pile o' pots can add up to a stunning yet practical vertical garden.

Vertical gardens and hanging baskets provide easy access from a standing or sitting position. Gene Rothert suggests building a wall garden: it's an upright wooden frame—four feet square (1.2 m²) is a good size—covered with black plastic and wire mesh. It is then filled with soil. The plants are inserted through slits cut into the plastic through the mesh (just like a giant grow-bag).

This could also be a free-standing structure mounted on casters for flexibility and accessibility from both sides. The Chicago Botanic Garden boasted a fabulous wall garden planted with parsley and heliotrope that looked like a hanging tapestry. For a more temporary arrangement, you could simply hang a series of grow-bags along a fence or wall.

An edible garden in a hanging basket makes harvesting a snap.

a mathematician studying chaotic (dynamic, unpredictable) systems such as weather. Doing a computer model of atmospheric currents, he found that the minutest discrepancy in initial conditions led to huge discrepancies later. (In another breakthrough, he also found that even chaos, on a larger scale, can produce ordered patterns.) As part of this holistic system, we can do a surprising amount of harm by spraying "just a bit of weedkiller here and there," but we can also do a surprising amount of good by tossing a few shovelfuls of compost on our plants. Just as the fly hitting one silken strand sends vibrations throughout the spider's web, so everything we do in the garden resonates through nature's web of intricate connections.

When we instill our hearts, minds and spirits into our gardens, whatever their size, shape or style, we create unique places for health and healing. Surrounded by abundant greenery, knowing about the thriving life beneath our feet, understanding more of the messages being passed invisibly from leaf to leaf and ant to ant, hearing the myriad tones that make up a deeper harmony, gaining appreciation for the smallest drop of rain and becoming aware of the rhythms that drive this great circle of life—we find the strength and balance to set things right in ourselves, our gardens and the larger world.

ENDNOTES

1 The Green Connection

[1] Harper, Peter, with Chris Madsen and Jeremy Light, *The Natural Garden Book: A Holistic Approach to Gardening.* New York: Simon & Schuster/Fireside, 1994. p. 124.

[2] *Human Genome Project,* The Wellcome Trust, Feb. 12, 2001. www.wellcome.ac.uk.

[3] Lewis, Charles A., *Green Nature/Human Nature: The Meaning of Plants in Our Lives.* University of Illinois Press, 1996. p. xvii.

[4] Wilson, Edward O., *Biophilia.* Harvard University Press, 1984. p. 1.

[5] *Ibid.* p. 101.

[6] *Ibid.*

[7] Malakoff, David. *What Good Is Community Greening?* ACGA 1998 www.communitygarden.org/pubs/whatgood.html.

[8] Mooney, P. and Nicell, P., "The importance of exterior environment for Alzheimer residents: effective care and risk management." *Health Care Management Forum,* 1992. p. 23.

[9] Olds, 1985, cited in Cooper Marcus, Clare and Barnes, Marni, *Healing Gardens: Therapeutic Benefits and Design Recommendations.* John Wiley & Sons, 1999. p. 8.

[10] Cooper Marcus, Clare and Barnes, Marni, *Gardens in Healthcare Facilities: Uses, Therapeutic Benefits and Design Recommendations.* The Center for Health Design, 1995. p. 38.

[11] Steven, M.L., and Armstrong, H., *The Congruent Garden: The role of the domestic garden in satisfying fundamental human needs.* International People-Plant Symposium, July, 1998, Sydney, Australia.

[12] Healthsourceuk, www.healthsourceuk.com/theragarden.

[13] Hughes, J. Donald, "The Psychology of Environmentalism Healing Self and Nature," 1991. *Trumpeter:* 8, 3.www.icaap.org/iuicode?6.8.3.2.

[14] Ibid.

[15] Leff, H.L., *Experience, Environment and Human Potentials.* New York: Oxford University Press, 1978. p. 13.

[16] Wilson, *Op cit.* p. 109.

[17] *Ibid.* p. 110.

[18] *Ibid.* p. 110.

[19] Moir Messervy, Julie, *The Inward Garden: Creating a Place of Beauty and Meaning.* Little, Brown and Company, 1995. p. 26.

[20] Kaplan, R., and Kaplan, S., *The Experience of Nature.* New York: Cambridge University Press, 1989.

[21] Corning, Peter A., "The Synergism Hypothesis: On the Concept of Synergy and its Role in the Evolution of Complex Systems." *Journal of Social and Evolutionary Systems,* 21(2) 1998, www.complexsystems.org.

[22] Capon, Brian, *Botany for Gardeners: An Introduction and Guide.* Portland: Timber Press, 1990. p. 53.

[23] Mosquin, Ted, "The Roles of Biodiversity in Creating and Maintaining the Ecosphere." *Ecocentrism,* 1999 www.ecospherics.net. Also published in *Biodiversity in Canada: Ecology, Ideas, and Action.* Stephen Bocking (ed.), Broadview Press. 1999.

[24] Jackson, Charles, *Native American Studies,* http://ucsu.colorado.edu/~jacksoca.

2 A Sense of Humus

[1] Logan, William Bryant, *Dirt: The Ecstatic Skin of the Earth.* New York: Riverhead Books, 1995. p. 7.

[2] Shapiro, Howard-Yana and Harrisson, John, *Gardening for the Future of the Earth.* Bantam Books, 2000. p. 77.

[3] U.S. submission to 5th Session of the United Nations, Commission on Sustainable Development, April, 1997. Available at www.un.org/esa/agenda 21/naHinfor/coutr/usa/.

[4] Bryant, *Op cit.* p. 28.

[5] Petrik, Vaclav, *Understanding the Soil Processes,* Petrik Laboratories. www.rain.org/~sals/Petrik.html.

[6] "Tetanus." *Microsoft® Encarta® Online Encyclopedia 2000* http://encarta.msn.com © 1997–2000 Microsoft Corporation. All rights reserved.

[7] Harvard Medical School's Consumer Health Information, www.intelihealth.com.

3 Water Ways

[1] Spa-Therapy.com. © 2000 Net Performance Commerce / HCB Associates. www.spa-therapy.com/history.htm.

[2] *Freshwater Series A-5* Published by authority of the Minister of the Environment, © Minister of Public Works and Government Services, 1999 Cat. No. En 37–81/5–1999E ISBN 0-662-18152-2 ©1996–2000, Environment Canada. All rights reserved. www.ec.gc.ca/water/en/info/pubs/FS/e_FSA5.htm.

[3] Environment Canada, www.ec.gc.ca/water/en/manage/use/e_facts.htm.

[4] Begeman, John, Pima County Urban Horticulture Agent, Oct. 30, 1998. "The Magic of Rain and Wildlife." *Arid Gardener,* http://ag.arizona.edu/hypermail/arid_gardener/2014.html.

[5] U.S. Geological Survey's Water Science for Schools, wwwga.usgs.gov/edu/acidrain.html.

4 In Praise of Trees

[1] Moerman, Daniel E., *Native American Ethnobotany.* Timber Press, 1998. pp. 11–12.

[2] Breuer, Georg, *Air in Danger: Ecological Perspectives of the Atmosphere.* New York: Cambridge University Press, 1980. http://healthandenergy.com/air_pollution_causes.htm.

[3] Nowak, David, *The Effects of Urban Trees on Air Quality.* USDA Forest Service, Northeastern Research Station, 1999. www.pcl.org/bonds/urbantrees.html.

[4] Nowak, David and McPherson, E. Gregory, United States Forests Service Northeastern Forest Experiment Station, 1993. www.westgov.org/wga/initiatives/tpl/sec17.htm.

[5] "Atlanta's Urban Heat Alters Weather Patterns." *Science@NASA.* 26 April 1999. http://science.nasa.gov/newhome/headlines/essol26apr99_1.htm.

[6] Xiao, Qingfu, McPherson, E. Gregory, Ustin, Susan L., Grismer, Mark E. and Simpson, James R., "Winter Rainfall Interception by Two Mature Open-grown Trees in Davis, California." *Hydrological Processes* 14, 763±784. 2000.

5 Variety Is Life

[1] Environment Canada, www.atl.ec.gc.ca/udo/primer7.html © Environment Canada. 2001. All rights reserved.

[2] *Weeds Gone Wild.* National Parks Service www.nps.gov/plants/alien/bkgd.htm.

[3] Environment Canada, *op cit.*

[4] Stein, Bruce A., Kutner, Lynn S. and Adams, Jonathan S. (eds.), *Precious Heritage: The Status of Biodiversity in the United States.* Oxford University Press, 2000. From the Executive Summary.

[5] Biodiversity Science Assessment Team, "Biodiversity in Canada: A Science Assessment for Environment Canada." Environment Canada, 1994. www.cciw.ca/eman-temp/reports/publications/biodiv-sci-asses/biodiv2.htm.

[6] *Ibid.*

[7] Lamoureux, Grégoire, "Edges." *Permaculture,* www.life.ca/nl/39/perma.html.

[8] Ingram, John, *When Cities Grow Wild: Natural Landscaping from an Urban Planning Perspective.* ©1998, 1999. Wild Ones—Natural Landscapers, Ltd. www.for-wild.net/whenciti/ingram-21.htm.

[9] *Hazardous Household Products.* Environment Canada. www.ec.gc.ca/soer-ree/English/1996Report/Doc/1-5-3-7-4-1.cfm.

[10] Johnson, Lorraine, "Cutting (Out) the Grass." *The Toronto Environmental Handbook,* 1999. p. 19.

[11] Kindra, G.S. "Perceived Relationship Between the Environment and Personal Health." *Communicating the Impact of Environmental Problems on the Health of Canadians: A Literature Review and Survey of Experts,* for Health Canada © Minister of Supply and Services Canada, 1992 www.hc-sc.gc.ca/hppb/ healthyenvironment/engpubs/impact/ciephc04.html.

[12] Fox, Roy, *The Impact of Chemical Lawn Care on Human Health.* www.eisc.ca/royfox1.html.

[13] Macunovich, Janet. *Fine Gardening,* No. 79, June 2001. p. 6.

6   Wild by Nature

[1] United States National Parks Service, www.nps.gov/plants/alien/bkgd.htm.

[2] Galbraith, David A. and Zavitz, Kate, Canadian Botanical Conservation Network, www.rbg.ca/cbcn/ en/library/homeowner.htl.

[3] Information from Canadian Poisonous Plants Information System. http://sis.agr.gc.ca/pls/pp/ poison?p_x=px, Texas State Department of Health and the National Safety Council, http://aggie-horticulture.tamu.edu/plantanswers/ publications/poison/poison.html.

7   Growing Organically

[1] Environmental News Network. 27 Dec, 2000. www.cnn.com/2000/NATURE/12/27/bird.deaths.enn/ index.html.

[2] Fox, Roy, *The Impact of Chemical Lawn Care on Human Health.* www.eisc.ca/royfox1.html.

[3] Environmental Illness Society of Canada. www.eisc.ca/pesticide_mor_part3.html.

[4] Olkowski, William, Daar, Sheila, and Olkowski, Helga, *The Gardener's Guide to Common-Sense Pest Control.* Newtown: Taunton Press, 1995. p. xiv.

[5] *Gardening for Life Fact Sheet.* www.goforgreen.ca/ gardening/Factsheets/Fact3.htm.

[6] Nardozzi, Charlie, "Fertilize with Epsom Salts." *NationalGardening.com.* National Gardening Association. http://gardening.about.com/ homegarden/gardening.

[7] Granatstein, David, "Suppressing Plant Diseases with Compost," From *The Compost Connection* newsletter, 1998. Good Fruit Grower. http://www.goodfruit.com/ archive/May1-98/special3.html.

[8] Ingham, Elaine, "Compost tea is a multipurpose elixir," *Fine Gardening,* April 2001. No. 78. p. 34.

8   Good Eating

[1] Rees, William, "Why Urban Agriculture?" Notes for the IDRC Development Forum on Cities Feeding People: A Growth Industry. 20 May 1997. *Urban Agriculture Notes, City Farmer.* www.cityfarmer.org/ rees.html.

[2] Saffron, Lisa, "Organic Food and Cancer Risk." Report for Bristol Cancer Health Centre. www.positivehealth.com/permit/Articles/ Organic%20and%20Vegetarian/safron30.htm.

[3] Davidson, Michael W., *The Phytochemical Collection,* ©1995–2001 by Michael W. Davidson and The Florida State University. All Rights Reserved. http://microscope.fsu.edu/phytochemicals/.

[4] Lloyd, Pauline, "Our Vegetable Heritage." *Vegan News,* www.btinternet.com/~bury_rd/heritage.htm.

[5] Yoon, Carol Kaesuk. "'Super' Plants are Safe: Study." *The New York Times,* reprinted in *Financial Post,* 19 March 2001: F6.

[6] Lively, Ruth, "Does Pressure-Treated Wood Belong in Your Garden?" *Kitchen Gardener* magazine #15, p. 55–59. www.taunton.com/kg/features/techniques/wood/3.htm.

[7] Christopher, Thomas A., "Weed." *Compton's Encyclopedia Online v3.0* © 1998 The Learning Company, Inc. www.comptons.com/encyclopedia/ ARTICLES/0175/01927680_A.html.

9 Please Step on the Thyme

1 Perry, Leonard P., "Fragrant Perennials OH 66." University of Vermont Extension System; Department of Plant and Soil Science, www.uvm.edu/~pass/perry/ohfragpe.html.

2 Grenier Simmons, Adelma, *Herb Gardening in Five Seasons.* Plume/Penguin, 1990. p. 271.

3 From *Rose Recipes from Olden Times* by Eleanor S. Rohde and Helen Kapp, Dover Publications, 1973. Thanks to Maureen Gilmer at www.gardenforum.com.

4 Minter, Sue, *The Healing Garden.* Headline Book Publishing, 1993. p. 60.

5 Grenier Simmons, *Op cit.,* pp. 251, 255.

6 *Incense Through the Ages.* www.lemurian-imports.com/spice/incenage.htm.

10 A Garden for the Senses

1 Landsberg, Michele, "Hope and Healing." *Gardening Life,* Early Spring, 2000. Vol. 4, No. 1. p. 94.

2 Doman, Robert J., "Sensory Deprivation." *Journal of the National Academy for Child Development,* 1984. Vo. 4, No. 3. www.nacd.org/articles/sensdep.html.

3 Funderburk, Laura, *What Is Colour.* www.insteam.com/LauraFunderburk/spectrum.htm.

4 Montgomery, Geoffrey, *Breaking the Code of Colour.* www.hhmi.org/senses/b/b140.htm.

5 Norfolk, Donald, *The Therapeutic Garden.* Cygnus Books, 2000. www.healthsourceuk.com/theragarden/intro/index1.html.

6 Wilke, Maxine, "Scent of a Market." *American Demographics,* August, 1995, © 1997 Cowles Business Media, www.demographics.com.

7 *Ibid.*

8 Perry, Leonard, *Fragrance in Flowers,* University of Vermont Extension. http://ctr.uvm.edu/ctr/press/00pressn40.htm.

9 Wilke, *Op cit.*

10 *Taste Matters,* International Food Information Council Foundation, http://ificinfo.health.org/insight/julaug99/tastematters.htm.

11 Barrable, Ross, *Listening to Harmonic Sound.* www.soundscapesinternational.com.

12 *Noise: How Loud Is It?* www.garlic.com/~pburnett/noise.htm.

13 *Now Hear This.* Youngstown State University Dept. of Environmental and Occupational Health and Safety, Oct. 14, 1998, http://cc.ysu.edu/eohs/bulletins/Hearing.htm.

14 "Noise Pollution." *The Columbia Encyclopedia, Sixth Edition.* © 2001 Columbia University Press.

15 *Absorption.* Info About the Dangers of Chemicals, http://members.aol.com/planetsolutions1/ps-moreinfo.html#toxic.

11 The Sky's the Limit

1 Kuhn, Monica, *Roof Greening.* Rooftop Gardens Resource Group, Toronto, Feb. 22, 1996. www.interlog.com/~rooftop/.

2 *About Green Roofs,* Green Roofs for Healthy Cities, www.peck.ca/grhcc/about.htm.

3 *Ibid.*

4 *Ibid.*

5 Kuhn, *Op cit.*

6 The London Ecology Unit, 1993, quoted in Velasquez, Linda *Exploring the Ecology of Organic Greenroof Architecture,* www.greenroofs.com/ecological.htm.

7 Kuhn, *Op cit.*

8 *Ibid.*

9 Lenart, Claudia M., *Gardens in the Sky.* July, 2000. *Conscious Choice,* © 2000–2001 Conscious Communications, Inc. www.consciouschoice.com/environs/gardensinthesky1307.html.

10 Fairholm, Jacinda, "Cities Feeding People," *CFP Report Series 25, Urban Agriculture and Food Security*

Initiatives in Canada: A Survey of Canadian Non-Governmental Organizations. www.idrc.ca/cfp/rep25_e.html#1.1%20%20Community%20Gardening.

[11] *Community Gardening: The Roots of Good Health.* Health Canada, © Health Promotion Online www.hc-sc.gc.ca/hppb/wired/gardening.htm.

[12] Rees, Willliam, *Op cit.*

[13] Nabhan, Gary Paul and Trimble, Stephen. *The Geography of Childhood: Why Children Need Wild Places.* Boston: Beacon Press, 1994. p. 75.

[14] Fairholm, Jacinda, *Op cit.*

12   The Healthy Gardener

[1] Ulrich, Roger. S. "Stress Recovery During Exposure to Natural and Urban Environments." *Journal of Environmental Psychology* 11, pp. 201–230.

[2] Blumenthal, James, *Effect of Exercise on Reducing Major Depression Appears to Be Long-Lasting,* Duke University Medical Center, 21 September 2000. www.dukenews.duke.edu/Med/exercise.htm.

[3] Miavitz, Elan Marie, "Grief Gardening: A Horticultural Therapy Program for the Bereaved." *Journal of Therapeutic Horticulture,* American Horticultural Therapy Association, Vol. IX, 1998, pp. 17–20.

[4] Turner, Lori, *Yard Work Builds Strong Bones.* University of Arkansas, 10 April 2000. http://pigtrail.uark.edu:80/news/2000/apr00/weeds.html.

[5] Blumenthal, James, *Aerobic Exercise Improves Cognitive Functioning of Older Men and Women.* Duke University Medical Center, January 15, 2001. www.dukenews.duke.edu/Med/jogbrain.htm.

[6] Friedland, Robert, *Active Life Helps to Ward Off Alzheimer's.* Case Western Reserve University School of Medicine and University Hospitals of Cleveland, OH. Study presented by American Academy of Neurology, 5 May 2000. http://newswise.com/articles/2000/5/ALZHEIM4.AAN.html

[7] Ainsworth, Barbara E., et al., "Compendium of physical activities: classification of energy costs of human physical activities," *Medicine and Science in Sports and Exercise,* pp. 71–80.

[8] *Something in the Air: Airborne Allergens,* The National Institute of Allergy and Infectious Diseases, February, 1998. www.niaid.nih.gov/publications/allergens/full.htm.

[9] Ogren, Thomas L., *Allergy-Free Gardening: The Revolutionary Guide to Healthy Landscaping.* Ten Speed Press, 2000. www.allergyfreegarden/com

RESOURCES

1   The Green Connection

Gerlach-Spriggs, Nancy, Kaufman, Richard Enoch, and Warner, Sam Bass Jr., *Restorative Gardens: The Healing Landscape.* New Haven: Yale University Press, 1998.

The Fibonacci Quarterly home page, http://www.sdstate.edu/~wcsc/http/fibhome.html

American Horticultural Therapy Association, 909 York St., Denver, CO 80206-3799. Tel: (720) 865-3616 www.ahta.org

Canadian Horticultural Therapy Association, 80 Westmount Road, Guelph, ON N1H 5H8. Tel: (519) 822-9842 www.chta.ca

2   A Sense of Humus

Nancarrow, Loren, and Hogan Taylor, Janet, *The Worm Book: The Complete Guide to Worms in Your Garden,* Ten Speed Press, 1998.

Stell, Elizabeth P., *Secrets to Great Soil,* Storey Communications, Inc., 1998.

The Soil Biology Primer, by the NRCS Soil Quality Institute, www.statlab.iastate.edu/survey/SQI/primer/index.htm

3   Water Ways

Caduto, Michael J., *Pond and Brook: A Guide to Nature in Freshwater Environments,* University Press New England, 1990.

Reid, Jeffrey, *How to Build Ponds and Waterfalls: The Complete Guide,* Tetra Press, 1998.

Rumary, Mark, *Xeriscaping: Planning and Planting Low Water Gardens,* Sterling Publishing Company, Inc., 2001.

4   In Praise of Trees

Brown, George E., and Bryan, John E., *The Pruning of Trees, Shrubs and Conifers,* Timber Press, 1995.

Dirr, Michael A., *Manual of Woody Landscape Plants: Their Identification, Ornamental Characteristics, Culture, Propagation and Uses,* 5th edition, Stipes Publishing Co., 1998.

Forster, R. Roy, and Downie, Alex M., *The Woodland Garden: Planting in Harmony with Nature,* Raincoast Books, 1999.

The Land Owner Resource Centre. www.lrconline.com

Treelink, www.treelink.org

5   Variety Is Life

Bocking, Stephen (ed.), *Biodiversity in Canada: Ecology, Ideas, and Action,* Peterborough: Broadview Press, 2000. www.trentu.ca/biodiversity

Grifo, Francesca, and Rosenthal, Joshua (eds.), *Biodiversity & Human Health,* Island Press, 1997.

Novacek, Michael (ed.), and Futter, Ellen V., *The Biodiversity Crisis: Losing What Counts,* The New Press, 2001.

6   Wild by Nature

Johnson, Lorraine, *100 Easy-to-Grow Native Plants for Canadian Gardens,* Random House Canada, 1999.

Pollan, Michael, *Second Nature: A Gardener's Education,* Dell Publishing, 1991.

Stein, Sara B., *My Weeds : A Gardener's Botany* (reprint), University Press of Florida, 2000.

Prairie Nursery, Inc., *Wildflowers & Native Grasses,* Westfield, WI. Tel: 800-476-9453. www.prairienursery.com

Wild Flower Farm, R.R. #3, Schomberg, ON L0G 1T0. Tel: 905-859-0286. www.wildflowerfarm.com

7 Growing Organically

Grissell, Eric, *Insects and Gardens: In Pursuit of a Garden Ecology,* Timber Press, 2001.

Nancarrow, Loren, and Taylor, Janet Hogan, *Dead Daisies Make Me Crazy: Garden Solutions Without Chemical Pollution,* Ten Speed Press, 2000.

Natural Insect Control. R.R. #2, Stevensville, ON L0S 1S0. www.naturalinsectcontrol.com

The Composting Council of Canada. 16 Northumberland St., Toronto, ON M6H 1P7. www.compost.org

The U.S. Composting Council, www.compostingcouncil.org

8 Good Eating

Seeds of Change, http://store.yahoo.com/seedsofchange

Seeds of Diversity Canada. P.O. Box 36, Station Q, Toronto, ON M4T 2L7 Canada. Tel: 905-623-0353. www.seeds.ca

Fukuoka, Masanobu, *The Natural Way of Farming: The Theory and Practice of Green Philosophy,* Japan Publications, 1985.

Weaver, William W., *Heirloom Vegetable Gardening: A Master Gardener's Guide to Planting, Seed Saving, & Cultural History,* Owl Books, 1999.

Golden Harvest Organics, http://www.ghorganics.com

9 Please Step on the Thyme

Bown, Deni, *Encyclopedia of Herbs & Their Uses,* Montreal: Reader's Digest Press, 1995.

Scoble, Gretchen, et al., *The Meaning of Herbs: Myth, Language & Lore,* Chronicle Books, 2001.

Richters Herb Specialists, Goodwood, ON L0C 1A0 Tel: 905-640-6677. www.richters.ca

10 A Garden for the Senses

Fehrman, Kenneth R., and Cherie, *Color: The Secret Influence,* Prentice Hall, 2000.

Mogelon, Ronna, *Wild in the Kitchen: Recipes for Wild Fruits, Weeds, and Seeds,* M. Evans & Company, Inc., 2001.

Worwood, Valerie Ann, *The Fragrant Pharmacy,* Alive Books, 1992.

11 The Sky's the Limit

Osmundson, Theodore, *Roof Gardens: History, Design & Construction,* W.W. Norton & Company, 1997.

Roald Gundersen, 507 Main Street, La Crosse, WI.www.mwt.net/~roald

Neighbourgardens, Rae Blewden, co-ordinator, www.cityfarmer.org/Neighborgardens.html

Caduto, Michael J., and Bruchac, Joseph, *Keepers of Life: Discovering Plants Through Native Stories and Earth Activities for Children,* Fifth House Publishers, 1994.

Kock, Henry, and Aboud, Steven, *A Life Zone Approach to School Yard Naturalization: The Carolinian Life Zone,* a resource manual published by The Arboretum, University of Guelph, 1996.

12 The Healthy Gardener

Adil, Janeen R., *Accessible Gardening for People with Physical Disabilities: A Guide to Methods, Tools and Plants,* Monarch Books of Canada, 1994.

Gardens for Every Body. University of Missouri-Columbia, www.muhealth.org/~arthritis/gardens

Gardenscape Tools. Catalog and mail order to Canada and U.S. www.gardenscape.ca

Rothert, Gene. *The Enabling Garden: Creating Barrier-Free Gardens,* Taylor Publishing Co., 1994.

INDEX

edge plantings, 60–61
edible flowers, 123
ellagic acid, 91
Emerson, Ralph Waldo, 1, 41
Enabling Garden, The (Rothbert), 145
endangered species, 56
epimedium (*Epimedium*), 49
Epsom salts, 82–83
euphorbia, 129
European ginger (*Asarum europaeum*), 127
Evelegh, Tessa, 106
Evergreen, 139–40
evergreens, 49–51
exercise, gardening as, 147–49
exotic plants, 68

false cypress (*Chamaecyparis*), 128
feather grass (*Stipa tenuissima*), 128
ferns, 49
fertilizers
    chemical, 19, 22, 63
    natural, 83–84
Fibonacci, Leonardo Pisano, 13
Fibonacci numbers, 13–14
fir (*Abies*), 128
fireweed (*Epilobium angustifolium*), 73
Florida dogwood (*Cornus florida*), 43
foamflower (*Tiarella*), 49
folic acid, 90
forbs, 70, 71
fragrance, 119–22
fragrant plants
    favorite, 122
    tips for growing, 122
Friedland, Robert, 148, 149
full spectrum harmonic sound, 14
fungi, in soil, 19

Galloway, Martin, 116

gardenia (*Gardenia*), 152
gardening aids, 154–57
Gardening for the Future of the Earth (Shapiro and Harrisson), 18
garlic, 82, 91, 104, 118
garlic mustard (*Alliaria petiolata*), 83
genetically engineered plants, 93–94
genetic diversity, 92–93
Geography of Childhood, The (Nabhan and Trimble), 138
geranium (*Pelargonium*), 107, 117, 126
ginkgo (*Ginkgo biloba*), 152
glory of the snow (*Chionodoxa*), 59
golden ratio, 14
gout weed, 74
grass clippings, 24
grasses, 38, 70, 151
green, 118
greenhouses, rooftop, 136
Green Nature/Human Nature (Lewis), 4
grief gardening, 147
ground beetles, 81
groundwater, 34–37
Gundersen, Roald, 136

hanging baskets, 156
harmony, 12–15
Harper, Peter, 2
Harrisson, John, 18
hay/straw, as mulch, 24
healing, defined, 2
healing herbs, 108–10
healing garden design, elements of, 9–10
healthy gardening, 146–57
    allergies, 149–54
    exercise, 147–49
    sun, 154
heat island effect, 46, 133
herbs, 38, 104–12

aromatic, 104–7
in containers, 112–13
creating herb garden, 110–13
culinary, 105
healing, 108–10
as insect repellents, 110–11
heritage seeds, 92–94
hickory (*Carya*), 128
Honeyman, Mary, 5
horizons (soil), 22
horse chestnut (*Aesculus hippocastanum*), 128
horticultural oils, 82
horticultural therapy, 7
hosta (*Hosta*), 69, 128
hover flies, 81
Hughes, J. Donald, 7
Human Genome Project, 4
hummingbirds, 85
humus, 21
hyphae, 19

impatiens (*Impatiens*), 60
Indian grass (*Sorghastrum nutans*), 70
indoles, 91
Ingham, Elaine, 84
Ingram, John, 61, 62
In Search of Nature (Wilson), 17
insecticidal soap, 82
insects. *See also* pests
    beneficial, 80–81
    herbs for repelling, 110–11
    plants for attracting/repelling, 101
    preventive measures, 79
    stings and bites, 153
invasive plants, 68, 73–74
Inward Garden, The (Messervy), 8
iris (*Iris reticulata*), 59
isoflavones, 91
isoflavonoids, 91

Japanese cherry (*Prunus serrula*), 127
Japanese maple (*Acer palmatum*), 59
Jekyll, Gertrude, 124
jetbead (*Rhodotypos scandens*), 49
Johnson, Hugh, 77
Johnson, Lorraine, 143
juglone, 51
juniper (*Juniperus*), 50, 129

Kaplan, Stephen and Rachel, 5
Kew Gardens, 93
Kniepp, Sebastian, 31
Kock, Henry, 43, 66, 140, 149
kudzu (*Pueraria*), 68
Kuhn, Monica, 134

labyrinth, 14–15
lacewings, 81
lady beetles, 80–81
lady's slipper (*Cypripedium*), 69
lamb's ears (*Stachys byzantina*), 30, 69, 126
lamb's quarters (*Chenopodium album*), 123
Landsberg, Michele, 115
landscape fabric, 25
larkspur (*Consolida*), 111
latex, 129
laurel (*Kalmia*), 49
lavender (*Lavandula*), 38, 59, 106–7, 121, 152
Lavender (Evelegh), 106
lawns, 37, 61–63
leaves, as mulch, 24
Le Corbusier, 132
Leff, H.L., 7
lemon balm (*Melissa officinalis*), 110
lemon-scented plants, 108
LeNotre, 62
Leonardo da Vinci, 14
Leopold, Aldo, 57, 94
Lewis, Charles, 4